Time Biases

Should you care less about your distant future? What about events in your life that have already happened? How should the passage of time affect your planning and assessment of your life? Most of us think it is irrational to ignore the future but completely harmless to dismiss the past. But this book argues that rationality requires temporal neutrality: if you are rational you don't engage in any kind of temporal discounting. *Time Biases: A Theory of Rational Planning and Personal Persistence* draws on puzzles about real-life planning to build the case for temporal neutrality. How much should you save for retirement? Does it make sense to cryogenically freeze your brain after death? How much should you ask to be compensated for a past injury? Will climate change make your life meaningless? Meghan Sullivan considers what it is for you to be a person extended over time, how time affects our ability to care about ourselves, and all of the ways that our emotions might bias our rational planning.

Meghan Sullivan is the Wilsey Family College Professor of Philosophy at the University of Notre Dame and the Director of the Notre Dame Institute for Advanced Study. Her work focuses on time, modality, value theory, rational planning and religious belief. She's published work with many leading philosophy journals and current serves as a co-editor for *Nous*.

‘Time-biased thinking can mislead us ... Sullivan’s arguments show that we should try reconsidering those kinds of intuitions-and that we should be wary, in general, of the strange places to which they can lead us.’

Paul Bloom, *The New Yorker*

‘Her book offers a unified explanation of the irrationality of all time-biases, seeks to explain their origins, and suggests some heuristics to help overcome them. It also includes illuminating discussions of the meaning of life, and of how one should feel about the prospect of an afterlife. The writing is exceptionally clear, and Sullivan engages readers with a mix of realistic vignettes and actual cases, many autobiographical, and all relating to issues that many of us will inevitably deal with: saving for retirement, planning sabbaticals, caring for an ailing loved one, etc.’

Tim Campbell, *Notre Dame Philosophical Reviews*

‘The best books in philosophy focus on new (or underexplored) problems and make significant headway in solving those problems. Sullivan’s Time Biases does exactly that. Her arguments are original, insightful, and usually compelling. Her understanding of the issues are so deep, and her writing so clear, that the careful reader can’t help but gain a significant understanding of the relevant philosophical terrain. This book is an invaluable contribution to the literature on time biases, which will hopefully grow in the future, thanks in part to this groundbreaking work’

Travis Timmerman, *Journal of Moral Philosophy*

Time Biases

A Theory of Rational Planning and Personal Persistence

Meghan Sullivan

OXFORD
UNIVERSITY PRESS

Great Clarendon Street, Oxford, OX2 6DP,
United Kingdom

Oxford University Press is a department of the University of Oxford.
It furthers the University's objective of excellence in research, scholarship,
and education by publishing worldwide. Oxford is a registered trade mark of
Oxford University Press in the UK and in certain other countries

First published 2018
First published in paperback 2023

Published in the United States of America by Oxford University Press
198 Madison Avenue, New York, NY 10016, United States of America

British Library Cataloguing in Publication Data
Data available

Library of Congress Cataloging in Publication Data
Data available

ISBN 978–0–19–881284–5 (Hbk.)
ISBN 978–0–19–288428–2 (Pbk.)

Printed and bound by
CPI Group (UK) Ltd, Croydon, CR0 4YY

Contents

List of Figures

Introduction

Time Biases

You are time-biased if you have systematic preferences about when events happen. For instance, you might prefer to spend your tax return now rather than save it for a rainy day, believing full well that if you put it in savings, it would increase in value. This is a near bias—caring less about the experiences money can buy when they are scheduled further in the future. You might prefer that a painful root canal scheduled for tomorrow was already over and done with. This is a future bias—caring less about an unpleasant experience when it's past. You might prefer that the best part of a vacation come at the end rather than the beginning. This is a structural bias—caring about the temporal sequence of your experiences. You might even have preferences about when events outside of the confines of your life happen. Perhaps you now prefer that environmental crises happen a long time after your death rather than in the next few generations, because imminent catastrophes would diminish the meaning of your projects. This is a kind of meaning bias—caring about when your life occurs in relation to other events.

Philosophers, economists, and social psychologists have tended to treat these time biases in a piecemeal fashion, offering different theories of the origin of such attitudes, different theories of how to measure their extent, and different verdicts on whether these various time biases are rational or irrational. But in this book, I will argue that our time biases are far more similar than we have acknowledged. And there is good reason to think that all time biases are irrational. Learning to recognize and overcome our irrational time preferences can help us become better planners. Indeed, if Plato is right, overcoming our time biases might even save our lives.

The book is divided into three parts. The first part (Chapters 1–4) will focus on whether it is rational to care less about events that would happen in your distant future. Many social psychologists and philosophers simply assume that near bias is a pervasive but irrational attitude. But why is it wrong to care less about the distant future? I will isolate two philosophical arguments for why near bias is irrational and defend the arguments against objections. In the process, I will also offer a theory of rational egoistic concern.

The second part (Chapters 5–7) will consider whether it is rational to care less about some events just because they've already happened. This attitude, while common, has been largely ignored by social psychologists and philosophers. I will offer a theory of what it is to discount your past, and then argue that such a time bias is irrational for the same reasons it is irrational to be near-biased.

The final part (Chapters 8–11) will develop a theory of why we are time-biased even though we shouldn't be. I will explain what is (and, more importantly, isn't) entailed by temporal neutrality. And I will show how this theory can help us in determining when to stick to our past plans, in planning for the future in the face of radical change, and in understanding the meanings of our lives even if none of our plans make a permanent difference to the world.

If your curiosity is piqued and you'd like to get straight into the debates about time biases, you can skip ahead to the first chapter. But some readers might be interested in a preview of the kind of rationality at play in these debates. The rest of this Introduction will describe the type of rationality that I am interested in, contrast it with some other common approaches, and then introduce the three main principles of rational planning that will reappear throughout the book.

What You Do vs. What You Prefer

This is a book about what you have most prudential reason to prefer and the extent to which temporal considerations should affect these preferences. Some philosophers—and many economists—think we ought to take our preferences as the fundamental inputs to a theory of rationality. On this view, there is no particularly deep question of why you have the preferences that you do. We just take it for granted that you have some preferences and then ask whether your set of preferences, taken as a whole, is logically consistent at a particular time. For instance, suppose Sparky the pyromaniac reports that right now he prefers blowing up cars to slowly burning them. But—Sparky immediately continues—right now he *also* prefers slowly burning the cars to blowing them up. The minimalists will deem Sparky irrational for having contradictory preferences. But they remain silent on whether there is anything irrational about wanting to torch vehicles in the first place.

We often have good reason to make sure our preferences conform to logical constraints. But we omit an important dimension of rationality if we take individual preferences to be immune from criticism. Rational beings can and should deliberate about what preferences they ought to have. And in deliberating about the reasons that back our particular preferences, we often come to realize that some of our preferences are irrational. For instance, I might start off the electoral year preferring that Bernie Sanders win the 2016 primary rather than Hillary Clinton, with little reflection on my reasons for this preference and not having formed any other electoral preferences. I find that I just like Bernie. This preference is logically consistent. But I might nevertheless find myself learning more about the various candidates' platforms and on the basis of new reasons come to prefer that Clinton win. There is an important sense in which my preferences are more rationally justified after this research and deliberation. And this improvement need not be explained as my preferences better cohering within some formal framework or with any of my other preferences. It has to do with my uncovering the reasons for what I should want. Philosophical reflection can help us uncover reasons for and against our preferences in just this way, and your preferences are more rational to the extent that they are better supported by reasons and less susceptible to bias.

Another major branch of philosophical work on rationality focuses on practical rationality—how we should determine our reasons for action. For instance, I might wonder if I have most reason to vote on November 3rd, or if I have most reason to stay home. Within this sphere, we may also draw a distinction between moral and prudential reasons. I may think I have the most moral reason to vote, since I think that universalizability is an important moral standard, and if everyone declined to vote, our democracy would fail. But I might also think that I have most prudential reason to stay home, since my individual vote will likely not make a difference to my future well-being, while staying home would allow me to sleep in an extra hour.

Aristotle thought that issues of prudence were only interesting insofar as our preferences relate to our actions: "Thinking itself moves nothing, but thinking that is for the sake of something and concerned with action does . . . Nobody now chooses to have sacked Troy in the past, and nobody deliberates either, about what has already come into being but rather what will be and admits of happening."[1] In this, he is not alone; many contemporary philosophers assume that issues of practical rationality are only interesting insofar as they pertain to rational action.[2] But in exclusively focusing on reasons for action, this concept of practical rationality also overlooks an important dimension of rational deliberation. We often deliberate about what we prefer the world to be like, even if we have no control over whether the world will be that way. For instance, I might deliberate about which outcome I prefer for the US presidential election, believing full well I have no control over the outcome. And often we deliberate about what we prefer while not really knowing how our actions might match up with these preferences. I may decide, for instance, that I prefer not to be kept on life support if I suffer a serious brain injury. But I might not know what course of action is best for realizing this preference. I may not even be able to bring myself to think now of any of the practical steps that realizing this preference would entail.

On the view of rationality investigated in this book, the preferences typically come first; the connection with action often comes later and sometimes not at all.[3] Here are five more examples of preference-focused rationality that will reappear in later chapters.

First, we can reason about our preferences for what the past could have been like. For instance, do you prefer your painful root canal to be over or to be still scheduled for a month from now? And what rational status do you give regrets—what should you prefer now about your past choices (and the preferences that guided those choices)? We have no control over the past, and this deliberation is not reasoning about what to do in the past. It is deliberation about what you prefer the world to have been like.

Second, we can deliberate about our personal post-mortem preferences. For instance, do you prefer that there be some form of spiritual afterlife? Or do you prefer that your natural death be the end of your existence? While we have control over whether we follow the precepts of some particular faith, we do not have any control over whether an

[1] Book 6, Chapter 2 of the *Nicomachean Ethics*.

[2] See for instance Chapter 1 of List and Pettit (2013) or Korsgaard (2009).

[3] Which is not to say I take any firm stand on the debate between causal and evidential decision theorists. The connections between such considered preferences and actions might be somewhat sophisticated, especially when facing Newcomb problems. For an overview of issues with translating "news value" accounts of rationality into rational decision-making, see Chapter 5 of Joyce (1999).

afterlife is possible or what such a continued life would entail. Still we can deliberate about what we want, even if we have no control over it. And such deliberation might indirectly influence decisions that we can control—for instance whether to attend a Catholic Mass or an atheist Sunday Assembly each weekend.

Third, we can deliberate about how we want the world to go after our deaths. Do you prefer that climate change hasten the end of human civilization, so you can be part of the last chapter of the human story? Do you prefer that there be many future generations after ours, who take an interest in the kinds of projects you cared most about in your life? You might not be able to hasten or delay the apocalypse, but you can form preferences about what happens outside the confines of your life, and, as we'll see, such preferences can play an important role in the kinds of projects you pursue now.

Fourth, we can deliberate about our preferences over scenarios we aren't sure are physically or biologically possible. A patient suffering permanent locked-in syndrome can deliberate about whether he'd prefer to run marathons or climb mountains. A space enthusiast can deliberate about which galaxy he'd prefer to visit, even in the absence of faster-than-light travel.

Finally, we can deliberate about our preferences over scenarios we aren't sure are metaphysically possible. For reasons related to their strange religion, the Pythagoreans strongly preferred that the square root of two be a rational number. Thomas Hobbes preferred that he be the scholar to discover how to square a circle. Both scenarios are metaphysically impossible, but not straightforwardly logically inconsistent. And both Hobbes and the Pythagoreans had reasons for their preferences—reasons a theory of rationality can weigh in on. We'll return to these issues in Chapters 5 and 7.

These kinds of deliberation are not only common, they are important to our agency and planning. Or so I shall argue here.

It would be useful to have a general name for the kind of rationality that concerns our reasons for wanting or not wanting different events to occur (or to have already occurred). For lack of a better term, I will call it *approbative rationality*—the rationality that governs what we should approve of happening.[4] As with practical rationality, we can

[4] There is an idea like approbative rationality in Richard Jeffrey's decision theory. He thinks we should model preferences over propositions in terms of the "news value" that comes from learning such states of affairs obtain. See Jeffrey (1983, 82–3). But unlike Jeffrey's

distinguish moral approbative rationality from prudential approbative rationality. Moral approbative rationality concerns your preferences given your moral reasons. Moral approbative rationality might require you to prefer a world where more wealth is redistributed to the actual world, because such a world would be overall happier. Moral approbative rationality might require you to prefer that World War I never occurred, even if you have no control over past wars. In contrast, prudential approbative rationality concerns reasoning about your preferences given your self-interest. Prudential approbative rationality might require you to prefer the actual world to a redistribution world, since you would likely lose money in a just redistribution scheme. Prudential approbative rationality might require you to prefer the actual world to one where World War I never happened, if the Great War was a precondition of your grandparents meeting and you eventually existing.

Approbative rationality isn't completely disjoint from practical rationality, because your reasons for action will tend to be based on your preferences, including ones that you've deliberated about. Furthermore, preferences that seem inert when considered on their own might be action-guiding when they are combined with your other beliefs and preferences. Indeed, many of the time-biased preferences we will discuss in the coming chapters have exactly this effect. What is distinctive about this approach is that we do not take preferences to be buried in us, waiting to be revealed by our choices. While complex features of our psychology might obscure some of our preferences, many of them—including some that are most important to who we are—are the sorts of attitudes that we can and should support with reasons. How exactly our preferences connect with our reasons will be a recurring topic in the chapters to come.

Three Principles for Rational Planning

This is a book about prudential approbative rationality, i.e. what preferences you should and shouldn't have insofar as you care about your self-interest. I will assume without much argument that there is a coherent

system, approbative rationality (1) focuses on reasons you might have for taking certain "news items" as preferable to others and (2) permits you to have rational preferences for metaphysical impossibilities.

distinction between self-interest, morality, and other kinds of normativity. I also agree with the philosophers and economists who think that rational preferences must be logically consistent at a time. This is a principle we can call:

Consistency: At any given time, a prudentially rational agent doesn't prefer states of affairs that are logically inconsistent.

Consistency gives one account of what's irrational about Sparky's automotive destruction preferences—they straightforwardly contradict one another. In other cases, preferences are broadly logically inconsistent because of what particular terms mean. For instance, someone who prefers both to stay vegan and to eat cheeseburgers fails the consistency test because being vegan *just means* abstaining from animal products.[5]

To the Consistency criterion, I add two more, which will be defended in the chapters to come. First, I assume that being prudentially rational should, in normal circumstances, mean preferring that our lives go as well as possible into the future. We learn about prudential rationality (and write books about it!) because we want to improve our lives and the lives of those who follow our advice. This motivates a principle that I call:

Success: At any given time, a prudentially rational agent prefers her life going forward go as well as possible.

In Chapters 2, 6, and 8, we'll clarify this principle and survey some arguments for and against it.

I also think that being rational means forming preferences and choosing actions that are supported by reasons. Indeed, the focus on reasons is characteristic of approbative rationality and motivates a principle that I call:

Non-Arbitrariness: At any given time, a prudentially rational agent's preferences are insensitive to arbitrary differences.

In Chapters 3, 7, and 8, we'll clarify this principle and survey some arguments for and against it.

[5] I will not, however, take consistency to rule out preferences over metaphysical impossibilities. Examples might include preferring the squared circle or a rational root of 2. And I won't assume that metaphysical impossibilities all reduce to forms of logical impossibility.

There are exotic cases where aiming at Success can seemingly conflict with Consistency and Non-Arbitrariness. For example, suppose an eccentric billionaire promises to bestow his fortune on you but only if you develop inconsistent preferences. Suppose further that he can somehow detect your preferences; maybe he is a brilliant psychologist or a telepath. In such a case, it seems you can't satisfy both Consistency and Success. Likewise we can imagine a problem case for Success and Non-Arbitrariness where the billionaire demands you form arbitrary preferences. We can even imagine a case where the billionaire promises a fortune only if you stop caring about your self-interest altogether, thereby making the Success criterion self-defeating.

How bad are such scenarios for an account of prudential rationality? We might avoid some of the conflicts by trying to reduce Consistency and Non-Arbitrariness to Success (or vice versa). Another option is to claim that they are independent but one of the rational standards always takes precedence over the others. A third option is to admit that we sometimes face rational dilemmas: planning problems where no matter what we end up partially failing.

I lean towards admitting that there are, occasionally, insuperable rational dilemmas—the eccentric billionaire problems being a paradigm. But I won't defend that in this book, and I won't argue for the supremacy of any of the three norms. Different arguments that I'll offer appeal specifically to versions of the Success or Non-Arbitrariness principles. The arguments can be taken separately if you find you accept one principle but reject the other.

Happily we rarely find ourselves faced with dilemmas involving billionaires fixated on spreading irrationality. Most problems of rational planning have solutions, and in many cases ensuring that your beliefs are consistent and non-arbitrary will help you to live better. Further, as a methodological point, in this book I'm committed to presenting real-world planning problems whenever feasible to make my argument. The theory on offer in this book should be tested against its ability to offer systematic and useful advice for how to form preferences in the face of actual planning questions just as much as it solves the puzzles of the philosophers.

You'll notice that the three principles discussed above apply to agents *at a time*. There are two perspectives you might take when you think about your plans and your self-interest. One is the *present perspective*—situated as you are now, in the present, are your preferences rational now and is your life going well from the present vantage point? Another is the *timeless perspective*—considering your life as a whole, is it a life rationally lived and a life that goes well? There is some philosophical disagreement about which perspective we ought to take when evaluating our plans. And the perspectives can offer conflicting verdicts about whether you are doing well. The arguments in this book will assume you are planning from the present perspective. That is, they will be posed to answer the question of what you should prefer now rather than what would be valuable from some timeless assessment of your life. I favor the present perspective approach for two reasons. First, as I will describe in more detail in Chapters 4 and 7, I think there are real and irreducible distinctions between the past, present, and future. We should not be so quick to abstract away from these differences when we consider our potential sources of reasons. Second, it is far more natural, I think, to be engaged in planning while also seeing your life as an event that you are in the middle of, remembering what happened, anticipating what will come next, and trying to point it in the right direction. So the temporal neutrality I will advocate does not require you to ascend to some timeless perch to be rational.

Acknowledgments

This book was initially dreamed up while on a year-long research sabbatical in 2015–2016. I am extraordinarily grateful to the University of Notre Dame, the Immortality Project, the New Directions in Time Project, and the John Templeton Foundation for supporting that year of research. I am also intellectually indebted to Preston Greene, Tom Dougherty, David Brink, and Derek Parfit. All four have done extensive, interesting work on temporal neutrality that has significantly guided my thinking. Chapters 5, 6, 8, and 11 draw in certain sections from research that Preston and I conducted together. His insight runs throughout those arguments (and is frequently cited). Chapters 3 and 7 draw in part from joint work with Peter Finocchiaro (likewise cited). Johann Frick and Tom Hurka offered very helpful suggestions during my visit to Princeton, which substantially shaped the direction of Chapters 5 and 6. The entire manuscript benefited extensively from feedback from my Spring 2016 graduate seminar on diachronic rationality: Elizabeth Anthony, Paul Blaschko, Rebeca Chan, Kate Finley, Liz Jackson, Ting Lau, Caleb Ontiveros, Callie Phillips,

Luke Riel, and Louise Williams. Notre Dame has a wonderful community of smart, creative, and relentless graduate students; I love sharing my work with them. Mike Rea, Tom Dougherty, and Ting Lau also gave extensive, extraordinarily helpful comments on the entire manuscript. Christine Grandy worked with me to design useful charts representing the various discount functions.

A version of Chapter 4 is forthcoming as an article in *Philosophical Issues*.[6] And a version of Chapter 11 is forthcoming as an article in the *Georgetown Journal of Law and Public Policy*.[7] I am grateful to both journals for their permission to reprint this material.

I am indebted to many departments and conferences for providing me venues to present portions of this book while it was in progress: the University of Iowa, NUS, NTU-Singapore, Syracuse, Hong Kong University, Lingnan University, the Centre for Time at Sydney, the ANU, the University of Manitoba, the University of Vermont, Rutgers, Duke, the University of Utah, the Notre Dame Law School, Princeton, UMSL, Brown, Columbia, the University of St. Thomas, the Georgetown Philosophy Department, the Notre Dame Center for Philosophy of Religion, the Immortality Project Capstone Conference, the Sydney Temporal Experience and Transformation Conference, the Iceland Future of the Study of Time Conference, the 2015 Rutgers Religion and Value Workshop, the 2016 Eastern APA, the 2016 Orange Beach Epistemology Workshop, the Georgetown McDonough Business School Conference on Remote Effects, the 2017 Desert Philosophy Workshop, the 2017 APA Pacific Pre-Conference on Transformative Experience, the 2017 Toronto Time in the History of Metaphysics Conference, the 2017 Milan Open Future Workshop, and the 2017 SPAWN Workshop in First-Order Metaphysics.

Most importantly, I am grateful to my family—Mary, Liam, Patrick, Ambrosia, and Connor—for teaching me humor, unconditional love, and that there is more to living than planning. This book is dedicated to them.

[6] Sullivan (Forthcoming a). [7] Sullivan (Forthcoming b).

1

The Received Wisdom

> "May we ask," said the ants, "what you were doing with yourself all last summer? Why didn't you collect a store of food for the winter?"
>
> "The fact is," replied the grasshopper, "I was so busy singing that I hadn't the time."
>
> "If you spent the summer singing," replied the ants, "you can't do better than to spend the winter dancing."
>
> Aesop, *The Fable of the Grasshopper and the Ants*

1.1 The Savings Struggle

Last year, I faced a decision. I'd saved up $3,000. I could put it towards my retirement account, or I could spend it to attend a friend's wedding in India. I was lucky to even have the decision—the vast majority of Americans do not have access to any employer-sponsored retirement plan and face crippling near-term expenses that make personal saving impossible.[1] I grew up in a family that lived paycheck-to-paycheck, and to this day my parents have little by way of savings. To some extent, my adult life has been defined by trying to overcome our family's anxiety about money and do a better job of planning for the future.

Which is to say, I try hard to base my savings preferences and activities on reasons. One hazard of being a philosopher is that I'm trained to seek out reasons: the pros and cons can quickly multiply.

I'm thirty-four right now. If I put the money in the retirement account, I won't be able to access it without penalties until I am sixty-five.

Pros: I am pretty confident that the index funds in my retirement account are a sound vehicle for saving money. If the "rule of 72" and

[1] See for instance Kim (2015) and Gabler (2016).

broad historical trends in the market hold fast—and I think they will—then $3,000 invested now will likely be worth almost $24,000 by the time I withdraw it. There is no way I'd spend that much money now on a trip to India (even taking the effects of inflation into account). So maybe I should save.

Cons: that happy withdrawal date is another lifetime from now! I live a (mostly) healthy lifestyle. I am confident I will survive that long. But I also think I will be quite a different person by the time I reach sixty-five. I will still like money, but my priorities will change. And I'm not presently very excited at the prospect of waiting thirty-one years in order to blow $24,000 on a downpayment for a seniors-only condo in Miami or a tranquil cruise down the Danube River. While I think I will highly value the condo or cruise *then*, I'd much prefer to spend the $3,000 *now* on the wedding trip. After all . . . it's India.

In the end, the prospect of adventure on the subcontinent was too much for me. I booked the trip. Was my decision rational, in the sense that it was properly supported by reasons? Or was I falling into the same spending trap that has been my parents' financial undoing?[2]

1.2 The Received Wisdom

The received wisdom is that individuals in my situation—healthy economy, healthy body, healthy love of money—ought to save. This wisdom is pressed upon us by entities with a clear institutional interest in our saving habits, especially banks and governments. In 2015 President Obama issued an executive order creating a Behavioral and Social Sciences Team to research how findings from behavioral economics and psychology might "be used to design government policies to better serve the American people." Saving is a civic virtue.

But we also tend to assume that saving is good because it is in our *self-interest*. That is, it benefits *us* to make short-term sacrifices for far-sighted gains. This assumption underlies the explosion of work in social and developmental psychology on self-control. From Walter Mischel's famous "marshmallow tests" to Roy Baumeister's work on the factors that affect adults' executive function to the current obsession with "grit" and

[2] This opening puzzle is reproduced in Sullivan (Forthcoming a).

perseverance and putting in 10,000 hours of practice. The last forty-odd years have found psychologists and economists fixated on the ways self-control manifests, the emotional mechanisms that influence its manifestation, and—most important of all—how it can best be taught. This obsession has yielded an explosion of quasi-academic "self-help" books with advice for those struggling to plan for their future.[3] In the introduction to Baumeister and Tierney's popular book on willpower we find the bold claim: "However you define success—a happy family, good friends, a satisfying career, robust health, financial security, the freedom to pursue your passions—it tends to be accompanied by a couple of qualities. When psychologists isolate the personal qualities that predict 'positive outcomes' in life, they consistently find two traits: intelligence and self-control. So far, researchers haven't learned how to permanently increase intelligence. But they have discovered, or at least rediscovered, how to improve self-control."[4]

I admit, I inhale these books. But as a philosopher, I repeatedly come back to the question of why. Why shouldn't children settle for the first marshmallow? Why am I making a mistake in not putting more money towards my retirement? Why is self-control in our self-interest? This book is my attempt to systematically answer these questions and others that, as far as I can tell, the psychologists have not thought to ask.

1.3 Discounting and Near Bias

To take a philosophical approach to the received wisdom, we should first make the claims a bit more precise. Another way to put the received wisdom is that it is irrational to have near-biased preferences. Near-biased preferences can be represented by a future-directed *temporal discount function*. A future-directed temporal discount function is a function in

[3] For instance Mischel (2014), Baumeister and Tierney (2011), Thaler and Sunstein (2009), Duhigg (2016), and Duckworth (2016).

[4] Baumeister and Tierney (2011: 1). Even more hyperbolically, Baumeister, Heatherton, and Tice open their more scholarly book *Losing Control* by declaring that "Self-regulation failure is the major social pathology of our time" (Baumeister et al. 1994: 1). Recently, there have been doubts about whether the mechanisms identified in this research are as robust as psychologists and economists would have us believe. See, for instance, the replicability problems for Baumeister's "ego-depletion" studies: Hagger and Chatzisarantis (2016).

which the values of good events decrease as they are scheduled further in the future. For bad events, the discount function increases as they are scheduled further into the future. For instance, given the choice between a routine colonoscopy now or one at next year's annual physical, a near-biased agent might prefer the one delayed by a year, especially if she isn't the sort of person to worry about the procedure in the intervening time. And given the choice between a certainly uncomfortable colonoscopy now or a slightly elevated risk of catastrophically painful colon cancer twenty years from now, a near-biased agent might prefer to wait and take her chances. But facing similar odds of cancer in the near future, she's likely to opt for the procedure.

To make our topic still more precise, a future discounter has a value function with three components:

(a) the amount of time between the present and some potential future event (typically an experience),
(b) the amount the discounter would value that event if it were present, and
(c) some discount function that relates the present value to the temporal interval. The function decreases (either continuously, discontinuously, or absolutely) if the value in (b) is positive. It increases if the value in (b) is negative.

The value function uses these inputs to determine your present, discounted value for that future event. For example, a "half-er" might be someone who discounts any colonoscopy by half if it is scheduled more than a year from now. You might be asked whether you prefer a two-hour colonoscopy today or a three-hour colonoscopy in eighteen months. If you are a half-er, you would prefer to wait. Even though the longer procedure would be an hour worse if it were happening *today*, because it is far enough away, today you value it about the same as an hour and a half procedure. (Note to readers already looking for reasons to delay important preventative screening: the average colonoscopy is much shorter than these thought experiment ones and, while uncomfortable, it need not be painful.)

If you don't have a discount function for future events, then you are *future-neutral*. A future-neutral agent might reason: "If I opt for the later procedure, in eighteen months I am going to have to pay the piper and that will be me suffering for three hours! I'd prefer any two-hour procedure now to any worse procedure in the future."[5]

Much of the work on the psychology of near bias has focused on discovering the discount functions for different sorts of goods—health, money, food, drugs, even scratching itches.[6] Another related research program in psychology and economics concerns the overall shape of our discount functions for the future. For instance, do we discount future good events exponentially or hyperbolically? An exponential discounter increases her interest in a future good at a steady rate as it gets nearer. In contrast, a hyperbolic discounter maintains a somewhat steady (and low) value until some good is very near, then her interest spikes. A hyperbolic discounter's curve is significantly more "bowed" than the curve of an exponential discounter, as seen in Figure 1.1.

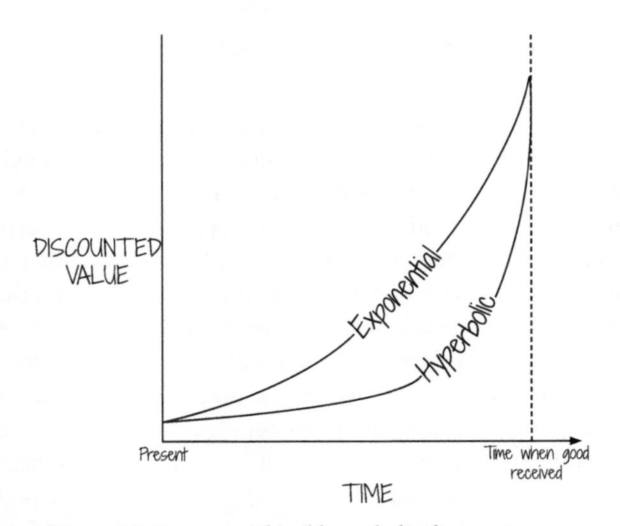

Figure 1.1 Exponential and hyperbolic discount curves

[5] Is anyone a future *increaser*? Such an individual would have a future markup function for (c), valuing good events more when they are delayed and valuing bad events even less. This could be a form of time bias, albeit a psychologically unrealistic one. While some of us might derive a lot of intermediate pleasure from anticipation of good events and extraordinary intermediate anxiety from anticipation of bad events, these emotions are not evidence that you have a future markup function for the events themselves. We will return to this when we discuss the connections between emotions and value functions in Chapter 8.

[6] For an introduction to this literature, see Loewenstein and Elster (1992).

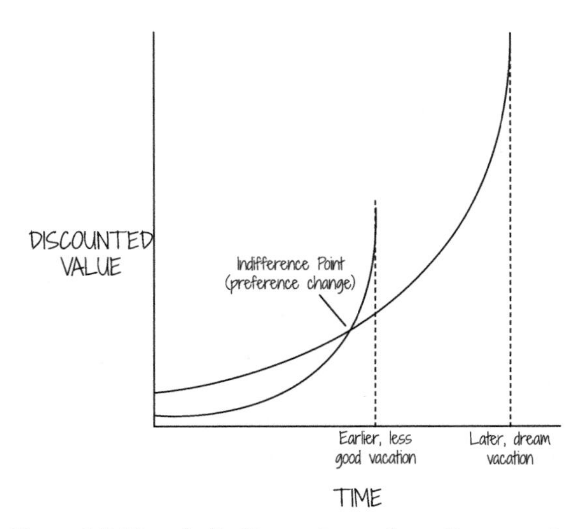

Figure 1.2 Hyperbolic discounting and vacation swapping

There is a lot of evidence that we are hyperbolic future discounters for most goods.[7] Hyperbolic discount functions are often thought to be especially problematic, because hyperbolic discounters will be willing to make inconsistent tradeoffs. For instance, suppose you are a hyperbolic discounter deciding whether you prefer a pretty good vacation sooner or a dream vacation much later. You may find that your discount functions for the two vacations cross before you have a chance to experience either of them. Why is this problematic? There will be a time before the smaller, sooner vacation when you will switch from preferring the sooner vacation to preferring the better, later one. Consider Figure 1.2, which represents a pair of hyperbolic vacation preferences. If I were a clever and shady travel agent, I might be able to take advantage of such a predictable preference reversal by offering you the option of choosing one vacation (for a small fee) before that time and then offering the option of switching back afterward (also for a small fee). As a hyperbolic vacation discounter, you will end up worse off because of your flip-floppy preferences than if you had just committed to one vacation choice from the beginning—you'll have paid me twice to end up exactly where you started. Exponential discount functions do not cross in this way.

[7] Ainslie and Halsam (1992).

Some philosophers—and many economists—think we can only criticize a future discounter if they have this pattern of reversible preferences. But as we'll see in coming chapters, there are strong philosophical arguments that having any future discount function (hyperbolic, exponential, or otherwise) is irrational.

1.4 Temporal Discounting and Risk Tolerance

You should take facts about uncertainty into account when planning for your future, and it is perfectly rational to sometimes prefer a smaller "sure thing" over a highly risky but potentially greater benefit. If you are deeply uncertain about your health, or the future of the stock market, or whether you'll become an ascetic in your sixties, then it might be irrational for you to sink large sums into a retirement account. But according to the received wisdom, if none of these uncertainties apply to you, then the mere fact that your retirement is such a long way off and that it is so tempting to spend the money sooner is no good reason to prefer keeping the funds liquid. You should try to overcome the emotions that lead you to think otherwise.

Risk discounting is especially important when we have to make a choice about how to act now based on our estimates of the value of an event and its likelihood. Indeed, theorizing about what choices are rational on the basis of such risk estimates is the focus of most work in decision theory. Risk discounting can be hard to tease apart from temporal discounting, since as events are scheduled further in the future, they tend to be more uncertain. For instance, in much of the follow-up work on the subjects of Walter Mischel's marshmallow test, a debate has raged over whether children from single-parent or poorer families (who are more likely to take the first marshmallow) are in fact forming their preferences based on their doubts that the experimenters will return with the second treat later. It is perfectly rational for a child who lives in a resource-insecure environment to assign a low probability to such promises.[8]

One rough way to tease apart probabilistic and temporal discounting employs a simple thought experiment that I call a reverse lottery.

[8] Sturge-Apple et al. (2016) offer evidence that such children are reasoning about taking the earlier reward in versions of the Mischel experiments.

To determine whether you are discounting some future event based on risk rather than time, imagine the event (and its salient consequences) happening sooner but with the same probabilities and same duration of causes and effects. For example:

> **"Pre-Paying" for Diabetes:** Mark is twenty years old and struggling to maintain a healthy weight. His doctor informs him that unless he has gastric bypass surgery now, he has a 20% chance of developing type 2 diabetes in the next fifteen years. The surgery comes with costs: Mark will require a highly regulated diet, will need to take nutritional supplements, and will not be able to drink alcohol ever again. But if he develops diabetes, there will be even more serious costs: Mark will develop chronic fatigue, vision problems, and frequent infections requiring hospitalization. If Mark is future-neutral, he'll think about the risk this way—would he be willing to enter a lottery tomorrow with the following options: (i) an 80% chance of living out the rest of his life diabetes-free with his current lifestyle, and (ii) a 20% chance of having to "pre-pay" for his lifestyle by developing diabetes immediately? Suppose if he loses the lottery, he'll suffer the symptoms of the disease and endure its treatments for the same duration he'd expect to suffer if he develops diabetes later in life. After that time, he'll be able to return to his normal lifestyle. If Mark isn't willing to enter such a lottery because the thought of a 20% chance of needing diabetes treatment tomorrow horrifies him, then he shouldn't put himself at such risk later in his life.

If Mark is unwilling to enter the lottery, then that is some evidence that it is the delay of the disease (not the risk) that explains his preferences. If he would be willing to get the gastric bypass surgery now to avoid facing such a lottery, future neutrality dictates that he ought to get it in the time-delayed case as well. This raises the important issue—one that will return again and again in this book—of how our emotions influence our attitudes towards the future. Our emotions are disposed to turn us on to nearby risks but not distant ones, and the temporal asymmetry of these emotions means that it is often harder for us to be motivated to appreciate distant risks. Reverse lottery thought experiments help us judge whether we are in fact comfortable with the risk involved in a plan or instead are being unduly influenced by asymmetries in our emotions. Of course, we cannot always account for all the salient consequences with the time reversal—for instance, we are ignoring the probability that Mark would die prematurely from his disease. But even with these limitations, reverse lottery thought experiments can often help us tease apart risk and time discounting.

1.5 Arguments for the Received Wisdom?

The received wisdom, from Aesop to modern social psychology, is that we ought to be willing to make present or near-future sacrifices in order to realize larger gains in the more distant future. The received wisdom favors future neutrality. Once you've calculated the probabilities of your retirement account appreciating or you potentially getting diabetes years from now, then *stop discounting*. Do not let the mere fact that these events will be a ways off influence your preferences. Such is the received wisdom, but are there any good arguments for it? And what assumptions about rationality underwrite the received wisdom? I think there are two major arguments for future neutrality, each with an interesting history and each originating from different but related views about what it is to be a rational planner. Developing and defending these arguments will be the task of Chapters 2–4.

2

The Life-Saving Argument

> The art of measurement . . . would make appearances lose their power by showing us the truth, would give us peace of mind firmly rooted in the truth, and would save our life.
>
> Plato, *Protagoras*

2.1 The Art of Measurement

The Knowledge is Power Program is the received wisdom about near bias institutionalized. KIPP is a system of charter schools across the United States, founded in 1994. KIPP schools are widely touted for their record of getting students in low socioeconomic status communities through high school and into college. Part of the KIPP program involves inculcating students with seven "character strengths" that will lead to success down the road, each represented with a cartoon icon on school posters. The icon for self-control is a marshmallow—a sly nod to Mischel's self-control studies. His early experiments focused on strategies children used to resist the temptation of taking a present treat (like a marshmallow) in order to earn a better treat later. Following up on their subjects years later, Mischel and his collaborators discovered that the ability to delay gratification in simple childhood tradeoffs predicts whether someone will realize more significant benchmarks later in life, like going to college, maintaining a healthy weight, and even sustaining a happy marriage. Such goods are plausibly taken to be in one's self-interest, broadly construed. Hence KIPP's focus on cultivating self-control strategies in their young charges.

As innovative as the KIPP curriculum seems, the Greeks had already discovered it some two millennia ago. For Plato, Aristotle, and many of their contemporaries, the point of learning virtue is to achieve a better life. A flourishing life is one with pleasure but also with certain forms of achievement, including knowledge, artistic accomplishment, deep friendships, athletic skill, and political power. Realizing such a life requires making calculated sacrifices and not being distracted by momentary impulses. Hence we find Plato extolling the importance of teaching the art of "weighing"—of calculating the appropriate values of events—lest we make imprudent tradeoffs. In the *Protagoras* he urges (in the voice of Socrates):

> Weighing is a good analogy [for planning]; you put the pleasures together and the pains together, both the near and the remote, on the balance scale, and then say which of the two is more . . . if you weigh the pleasant things against the painful, and the painful is exceeded by the pleasant—whether the near by the remote or the remote by the near—you have to perform that action in which the pleasant prevails . . . While the power of appearance often makes us wander all over the place in confusion, often changing our minds about the same things and regretting our actions and choices with respect to things large and small, the art of measurement in contrast, would make appearances lose their power by showing us the truth, would give us peace of mind firmly rooted in the truth, and would save our life. (356b–e)[1]

The "save our life" line is not hyperbole.[2] Earlier in the dialogue, Socrates compares the survival fitness of humans to that of animals, and he notes that with our relatively meager natural advantages, we depend heavily on our intellectual advantages. We have to husband our resources and organize politically, two achievements that require forward thinking. The ants in Aesop's fable survive the winter because they are adapted in just these ways, while the grasshopper suffers for his lack of appropriate foresight.

Plato doesn't think that near bias is irrational only insofar as it drives us to make imprudent tradeoffs. He also thinks that rationality requires having preferences now that fit the appropriate values of both near and distant future events. In the *Philebus*, Plato urges that it is important in and of itself to have the proper reactions ("true pleasures") when contemplating tradeoffs (41e–42c). The spendthrift who fails to plan for his retirement is not only making a bad tradeoff. His current preferences are poorly reasoned, since he has most reason now to want to have stable finances in his old age. Aristotle takes up this point as well in *De Anima*,

[1] Plato (1997).

[2] For discussion of the art of measurement in *Protagoras* and *Philebus*, see Chapter 5 of Warren (2014).

arguing that one feature that separates men from animals is our ability not only to engage in imagination about future pleasure and pain but to measure those pleasures and pains (whenever they are scheduled) against a fixed standard (3.11 434a6–15).

On this view, near bias results from a kind of ignorance about the proper value of goods scheduled in the future. We might contrast this with the broader definition of near bias offered in the last chapter. There we defined a near-biased agent as anyone who employs a future-directed discount function. This discount function may be a result of present ignorance about the value of future experiences (when they would be experienced). Or it may be the result of a fully informed diminishing concern for the future.

The wisdom of the Greeks holds for us as well. Consider, for instance, the large number of home buyers in the early 2000s whose lives were derailed because they failed to anticipate the true future costs of their adjustable-rate mortgages. Or the smokers who fail to adequately anticipate the suffering caused by lung cancer. There are certain planning problems that each of us faces where failure to appropriately measure the future can have ruinous effects on our lives.

2.2 The Life-Saving Argument

We can make the Plato-inspired argument for future neutrality more succinct and precise. Let's call a *distant tradeoff* any situation where someone faces a choice between a present good and some future good that (i) would be greater than the present good when it would be experienced, but (ii) is delayed enough to (now) be valued less than the present good given the agent's discount function. An example of a distant tradeoff might be deciding whether to invest $3,000 into a retirement account. I forgo whatever goods the money would buy now for the goods that the $24,000 will buy in thirty-one years. I assume those goods will be much better when I can finally access them. But if I am near-biased, I may presently value the investment less than $3,000.

Here is the argument:

The Life-Saving Argument for Future Neutrality

(1) At any given time, a rational agent prefers that her life going forward go as well as possible. (The Success principle)

(2) If you are near-biased, then in distant tradeoffs you will prefer and choose the present, lesser good over the greater, future good.
(3) Your life going forward would go better if you preferred and chose the greater, future good in a distant tradeoff.
C. So near-biased preferences are not rationally permissible, insofar as you face a distant tradeoff choice.[3]

What do we mean by a "good" here? This is a contentious issue, even among the Greeks. We might think of the good in question as subjective pleasure; the problem with near-biased agents is that they end up having experienced significantly less pleasure over the course of their lives. We might also think of the good in question in terms of desire satisfaction: near-biased agents trade future opportunities to satisfy greater desires in order to presently satisfy lesser desires. We might also think of the goods in a more "eudaemonistic" way. Eudaemonistic thinkers hold that there are at least some measures of well-being that cannot be reduced to pain, pleasure, or desire satisfaction. For example, becoming a parent or receiving an education might not satisfy any of your desires or make your life more pleasurable, but these achievements can count towards your life going well. On the eudaemonist approach, near-biased agents are criticizable because they miss out on accomplishments that require sustained investment and sacrifice. There are also hybrid positions, most notably John Stuart Mill's. Mill held that we are ultimately after experiences of pleasure but as a matter of course people with flourishing lives (in the eudaemonist's sense) tend to realize significantly more pleasure, since as we develop our higher faculties, our pleasures are of a higher quality.[4] There are also value pluralist positions, which hold that there are distinct, irreducible categories of goods we could aim at in a life.

There is an interesting debate about what exactly the goods are that self-interested agents ought to aim at. But we do not need to take a stand on the nature of the relevant goods here, since we face distant tradeoff

[3] We will assume that preferences fall into one of three categories: rationally permissible, rationally obligatory, or rationally impermissible. If your preferences are not rational at a time, they are rationally impermissible at that time.
[4] Chapter 2 of Mill (1863).

scenarios for any of them.[5] To keep matters simple, I will tend to focus on hedonic tradeoffs in the arguments in this chapter and the next. When appropriate, we'll generalize to other goods.

Is the Life-Saving Argument question-begging? The Success principle entails that a rational agent care that her life going forward go as well as possible. You might worry that, as stated, this principle assumes future neutrality, since it requires concern for future success. But Success alone does not entail future neutrality, because the Success principle alone is silent with respect to how we define the future good. Some (admittedly odd) ways of defining Success are consistent with future discounting. For instance, suppose you were a *tragedian*: you believe your life will go best overall if it will end with a period of very low well-being. As a result of your view of Success, you prefer any goods sooner and any suffering to be delayed, since such scheduling will make your life more tragic. Nobody is a tragedian. But as we will see in Section 2.5, there are substantive questions for how the scheduling of events affects measurements of well-being over the course of a life.

Is the Life-Saving Argument sound? Premise (2) follows from how we have defined what it is to be near-biased and to face distant tradeoffs. We assume that absent any moral side constraints, you will choose at a time based on your preferences at the time. Premises (1) and (3) are where the philosophical dragons lurk. Let's consider some objections to these premises, and in the process get more clear on why adopting a success standard for prudential rationality precludes future discounting.

2.3 Rationality Doesn't Require You to Care?

The Life-Saving Argument assumes that being prudentially rational entails preferring now that you do well going forward. You might object to this premise insofar as it places a substantive constraint on what preferences a rational agent ought to have. Some philosophers—and many economists—think that a theory of prudential rationality should not be in the business of assuming anything particular about what we should prefer. It should just be in the business of telling us whether our

[5] But there is a question of whether we are in fact disposed to be near-biased for more eudaemonistic goods. See Section 5.2.2 of Hurka (1996) and Chapter 5.

preferences are satisfiable in some logical framework, whatever those preferences may be. For instance, rationality requires that preferences be transitive—if you prefer burning all of your money to hiding it, and you prefer hiding your money to investing it, then you had better prefer burning your money to investing it. But rationality is silent on whether the best financial plan involves gasoline, camouflage, or mutual funds. This view is sometimes called Humeanism about prudential rationality, because in his *Treatise of Human Nature* David Hume claims: "Where a passion is neither founded on false suppositions, nor chooses means insufficient for the end, the understanding can neither justify nor condemn it . . . Tis as little contrary to reason to prefer even my own acknowledged lesser good to my greater . . . " (2.3.3.6).

Hume seems to deny the first premise of the Life-Saving Argument, but there is an open question of how exactly we should interpret his claim. We might think that Hume is claiming there is nothing criticizable in you preferring that things not go well for you. This interpretation is odd, given that later in the *Treatise*, Hume is more than happy to criticize near-biased agents: "There is no quality in human nature which causes more fatal errors in our conduct, than that which leads us to prefer whatever is present to the distant and remote, and makes us desire objects more according to their situation than their intrinsic value" (3.2.7.8). In this passage, Hume echoes Plato: near bias is a manifestation of a mistake in how to value distant goods. If an agent does not care about the shape of her whole life because she cannot appropriately appreciate the value of far-off events, then she is criticizable, because her preferences are based on false suppositions about value.[6]

But suppose you aren't making a near-sighted mistake in determining the value of distant goods. And suppose you nevertheless insist that you just don't care about how well your life goes. Can you still be criticized? The Life-Saving Argument will not have any grip on the neo-Humean who insists he is not making any error in valuation. The received wisdom about prudence presupposes a view of rationality that is more substantive than the Humean one. If you are the kind of person who in fact cares about how your life goes, then you ought to be future-neutral. But if you're already an extreme and unrepentant neo-Humean, then I suspect much

[6] For discussion, see Weller (2004).

of the rest of this book is unlikely to persuade you of anything. Happily, I think many of us are moved by one or another of the above considerations and do think there is something to the received wisdom.

2.4 Bookstore Buddhism

You might also take issue with the Success principle because you think that the holistic principle, if taken seriously, would lead us to miss out on many significant goods in life. I teach large groups of freshmen in Introduction to Philosophy at Notre Dame. My students are remarkable in many ways, but I still worry about them. They are so focused on the future—their grades, their major, their summer internships, their job prospects—they tend to miss out on the day-to-day opportunities that come with being a newly liberated adult. They don't take time to read for fun, to appreciate their relationships, or to savor their accomplishments thus far. The process of navigating the college rat race makes some of them miserable. And for a small number of them, the stress threatens the rest of their lives.

Is all of this focus on planning leading them to worse living? There is a worldview we might call "bookstore buddhism," which holds that the best thing to do is live in the moment. The advice is promulgated in any number of contemporary self-help books and bears only a passing relationship to real Buddhist traditions (many of which do not even countenance a self to help). According to the bookstore buddhist, focusing on maximizing the goods in your whole life is self-defeating. To live your best life, you should find satisfaction with the goods of the present moment.

It is interesting how little discussion (or funding) we see proposing to create KIPP-equivalent schools that encourage the young to seize the first marshmallow they see. But surely there is something to the view underlying bookstore buddhism. There are several ways we might understand the claim that you should live in the moment, and all of the most plausible interpretations are consistent with the Success principle.

First, we might understand "live in the now" as a strategy for extracting as much value out of present events as possible. When I worry about my over-scheduled freshmen, I worry that they are failing on this front. Exciting events are happening in their lives now, but they are either too uninformed, too nervous, or too myopic to enjoy them properly.

And some of these experiences will never be available to them again. It is perfectly consistent with future neutrality to recommend that *when* events occur, we actually realize their value. The art of measurement is an art of appreciating the true value of things. Learning this art will involve cultivating mindfulness of present experiences.

Second, we might understand bookstore buddhism along the lines of Horace, who famously entreats his readers *carpe diem!*—to seize the day. The advice seems to be to prefer (and act on) the opportunities available to you now rather than hedging in the hopes of some later good. *Carpe diem* may seem at odds with the Life-Saving Argument, but in the next line of his *Odes* Horace offers us the reason why we should seize the day: *quam minimum credula postero*—put little trust in the future (1.11.8). If we are very uncertain of the future, we account for this using probabilistic discounting. And so Horace's adage is equivalent to the (far less snappy): *appropriately weigh future uncertainty!* Most of us are, happily, not so skeptical about our future prospects. So if uncertainty is the only reason to seize the day, this will be accommodated by probabilistic discounting when we deliberate about how to act. If uncertainty *isn't* the reason to seize the day, then we need some other account of why our ambitions should be so focused on the present—a reason Horace does not provide.

Third, we might understand the bookstore buddhist as resisting the persistent encroachment of future concerns. We might think that younger future-neutral agents, like my beleaguered freshmen, could likely *always* expect greater overall returns if they delay gratification, given the vast number of investments available to them that are likely to appreciate in the long run. But a life of constantly deferred gratification is a life badly lived. We can imagine a young person who forgoes every present luxury in order to contribute to her retirement account. She can expect a healthy return on her investment. But such a miserly life falls far short of ideal. Sometimes, you need to treat yourself.

Future neutrality does not entail this miserly approach to pleasure or any other goods for that matter. Psychological facts about diminishing marginal utility will eventually recommend against saving every last cent you earn for the end of your life—each additional contribution to your retirement account is buying you less good for your buck on the withdrawal day. Spending a thousand dollars as a poor student will likely make you very happy. If you've already saved two million dollars, an extra thousand won't have much impact. Future-neutral agents don't discount distant experiences, but they do not inflate their value either. A future-neutral agent who experiences diminishing margins will likely try to distribute goods across her life.

There is a hypothetical puzzle that future-neutral agents will face. To see the puzzle, consider an (admittedly silly) thought experiment. Suppose Eternal Eddie will live an infinitely long life. And suppose God offers Eddie the promise of a single experience of bliss at one time in his life. Further, God promises that for every day Eddie waits to schedule the bliss, God will make the bliss even better. Poor Eddie; if all he cares about is blissing out as much as possible, he'll never schedule his bliss. This is a version of the paradox of the infinite positive return.[7] This paradox has nothing to do with the real-world distant tradeoffs faced by finite creatures like us. And it doesn't impugn future neutrality directly. What it does suggest is that when we deliberate about how to *act* on our preferences, we should take our anticipated future preferences into account. If Eternal Eddie knows he'll be constantly presented with the increased bliss offer, and he knows his preferences will remain future-neutral, and he knows he prefers to realize some bliss rather than none, he will choose to accept one of the offers. While he might not be rational in preferring one particular offer over a slightly later one, he could be rational in acting to choose an offer. In Chapters 3 and 6 we will revisit this issue of how rational agents should take their future preferences into account in more ordinary decision puzzles.

2.5 Measuring a Whole Life

What about Premise (3) of the Life-Saving Argument, the premise that your life as a whole would go better if you received the greater good? How do we measure whether a life "as a whole" is going better or worse?

There are at least three broad approaches we might take to this question. The first, we might call the *simple* approach. According to the simple approach, the value at any interval in a life is determined by what happens in that interval (internalism), and the good of a whole life is simply the sum of the goods realized in each of the intervals that compose it

[7] Koopmans (1965) calls this "the paradox of the indefinitely postponed splurge." Also compare the problem to Arntzenius et al.'s *Trumped* (2004: 252).

(additivity).[8] For example, suppose Joe lived thirty years. The first decade did him about 80 units of happiness. The second gave him 100. But the third only gave him 20. On the simple approach, Joe's life would be just as good as someone who lived forty years and each decade conveyed 50 units of happiness. Both lives convey 200 units of happiness value overall to the individuals who lived them. On the simple approach, the distribution of the value across a life is irrelevant.

The Life-Saving Argument is plausible on the simple approach to measuring the value of a life, since the near-biased agent prefers a whole life with a lesser good replacing a greater one. So she prefers a whole life with less value.

But not every philosopher is satisfied by this algorithm for calculating the value of a life. For instance, the simple approach seems to give rise to what Larry Temkin calls the "single life repugnant conclusion." Suppose you are given the choice between two lives. Option 1—the Short Life—would last 100 years, each year giving you 100 units of value. Let's suppose that's the equivalent of living each year healthy, loved, secure, and with many interesting opportunities. Option 2—the Very Long Life—would last 11,000 years, each year giving you just 1 unit of value. It is hard to imagine what such a life would be like, but let's suppose it would be one where each day was barely worth living. It is a life of insecurity, few meaningful relationships, poor health, and scant opportunities. Simple additivity says you ought to prefer the Very Long Life to the Short Life, since the Very Long Life conveys 11,000 units of value overall, while the Short Life conveys only 10,000. More generally, on the simple approach, for any possible finite life, no matter how much longer or how high the average quality of that finite life must be, there must be some much longer imaginable life which, if other things are equal, would be better, even though each period of that life would be barely worth living.[9]

Counterexamples like these might motivate more complex approaches to weighing the value of lives.[10] We might, for instance, deny the additivity assumption. On the *structural* approach to measuring the value of a

[8] Similar to the setup in Bradley (2011).

[9] Temkin (2012: 119). The problem was originally identified by McTaggart (1927). McTaggart doubted we could imagine scenarios like Very Long Life, and so doubted we could trust our intuitive preferences in this thought experiment.

[10] For a sophisticated overview of life aggregation issues, see Broome (2004).

life, facts about the order of goods in a life can affect the value of the life as a whole. Structuralists might maintain that a shorter life with highs is a better structure than a low, long life. Given the difficulty of imagining the long, low life, you may not trust your judgments about its value. But structuralism also weighs in on more realistic kinds of lives. For example, suppose you had a choice between one of two possible ways your life could go. One is to have a life of gradually increasing well-being at times, starting off small and getting larger and larger. Another is to have a life of gradually decreasing well-being at times, starting off with events that confer a lot of well-being, but ending with events that confer little. Even if the total sums of well-being across the lives were the same, you might still prefer a life that "keeps getting better" to a life that "keeps getting worse." If this is your reaction to the case, then you have a structural time bias. You are biased with respect to the earlier–later relations that hold between events.[11] In response to the single life repugnant conclusion, the structuralist might insist that while the Very Long Life contains more aggregate value than the Short Life, we should discount the Very Long Life because it has a far worse structure.

What could justify preferring one life structure over another? You might think that certain lives (i.e., the constantly improving ones) have better stories. This is a *narrativist* version of structuralism—structure matters insofar as it matters to have a life with a particular narrative value.[12] Narrativists should presumably impose some additional, objective constraints on which kinds of stories a rational person should aim for. For instance, consider the following true story of a felon with strange narrative preferences:

> **Number 33:** In 2005, Eric James Torpy reached a plea agreement with prosecutors to serve a thirty-year prison sentence for robbery and shooting with intent to kill. Torpy is an avid fan of Celtics basketball player Larry Bird. Bird's jersey number was 33. Torpy requested—and was granted—a three-year extension of his sentence so that he could "go down in Larry Bird's jersey."[13]

[11] See Section 128 of Moore (1903), Chapter 4 of Lewis (1955), Section 61 of Brentano (1973), and Velleman (1991).

[12] Following terminology in Bradley (2011).

[13] Associated Press, "Felon Gets Longer Sentence to Match Bird Jersey." October 20, 2005. Thanks to Peter Finochiarro for suggesting the case.

Torpy is presumably irrational in preferring to extend his suffering in prison merely so that he might have a life where he serves a sentence corresponding with Bird's jersey number. Not every story is worth striving for.

Perhaps we might assume that a life with a story of success (i.e., one where worthy projects are completed) always has more value than a life without such a story. Even with these constraints, what should a prudent person aim at overall? Should you aim to have the best future possible? Or should you aim to have a life with the best story of success possible? And what should you do when these considerations conflict? For example:

> **Golden Years:** Frank is approaching retirement. He has spent most of his career working on a book, and if he threw himself into the project, he could finish it. But he gets little pleasure from the project anymore, and he thinks he would be happier if he abandoned the book and spent his golden years playing with his grandchildren. Suppose that a life where he finishes his book has more narrative value than one where he spends the rest of his life playing children's games. Success would recommend abandoning the project. Concern for narrative value would recommend finishing the project. Which plan is more prudent?[14]

Maybe the best bet is for the narrativist to maintain that there are two kinds of value at play—value having to do with happiness going forward and narrativist value. The prudent agent should weigh them against each other, adding up the narrative and future-looking values of the lives on each option and preferring the one that comes out as more valuable. But this approach leads to some strange and rationally suspect anticipated preference reversals. For example, at the end of his career, Frank no longer has any future-directed value from the book. But at the beginning of his career, with so much life ahead of him, these happy golden years weigh far less in the future-directed calculation. The narrative value of each life option stays fixed over time, with the life where he finishes being somewhat more valuable than the one where he gives up. Following the "directly compare narrative and future-directed happiness" approach, Frank would be rational in committing to stick with the book at the start

[14] This puzzle case for narrativism has a structure similar to one in Bradley (2011).

of his career. But by the end of his career, the rational thing to do would be to abandon it. Moreover, at the start of his career, Frank would be able to *predict* that sticking with the book is only temporarily the rational thing to do. He would be certain at the start of his career that by the end he'd abandon his project. How could rationality license such flip-flopping? And why would you start a significant investment (like writing a book) if you were certain you'd abandon it at the end?[15]

The narrativist might respond by arguing that only the narrative considerations matter. Note that this has some surprising implications. Agents like Frank, at the end of their lives, would have reason to finish projects even if they'd get no happiness from the projects going forward. We'll return to these consequences for narrativism in Chapter 9.

We might also question the internalist assumption made by the simple approach to calculating the value of a life. On the *externalist* approach, facts about what happens outside of a certain interval of time can contribute to the goodness of that interval. Solon (and, arguably, Aristotle) held views like this about well-being. Solon famously cautioned King Croesus "count no man happy until the end is known," the idea being that a later reversal of fortune can make earlier events in a life better or worse. For instance, maybe you just received a big promotion at work. You think, "this is a great year for me—I'm finally in the upper management!" But next year you discover your company has been involved in massive fraud. Even though you played no part in the misdeeds, you are ruined. In retrospect, the promotion year was worse for your overall life than you thought. This is not because of any spooky backward causation. The scandal does not change any facts about what you experienced the previous year. But it changes the meaning and context of those experiences. And to the extent that meaning figures into the value of an interval of time in your life, the value of any particular interval is hostage to facts about what comes before or after it. Indeed, there is psychological evidence that we assign meaning only to events that have already transpired—i.e., meaning assignments (unlike pleasure assignments) tend to be retrospective. We'll return to this issue in Chapter 11.

I am not sure which of these approaches is the best method for calculating the value of a life, and, as mentioned in Section 2.2, I hope to remain

[15] We'll return to issues of anticipated preference reversal in Chapters 6 and 9.

neutral among the different accounts of well-being. What is important for our purposes is that on *any* of the major theories for calculating the value of a whole life, Premise (3) of the Life-Saving Argument is plausible. To accommodate structuralism, we need only assume that the relevant tradeoffs do not involve any significant structural changes to a life. (Or we can make "prefer a life with the best story" another principle of rational planning, alongside Success and Non-Arbitrariness.) Likewise, if the externalists are right, then we must assume that the relevant distant future tradeoffs do not adversely affect the value of other moments of your life. As a matter of course, most of the "good" structures of a life championed by the structuralists and externalists emphasize lives ending well, so this is unlikely to be an issue.

You might agree with all of this, but still wonder, what makes some events part of *your* life, the kind of life you are most interested in when you plan for the future? Does the Life-Saving Argument presuppose that we have temporally unified lives? This will be a major theme of the next two chapters when we encounter the second main argument for future neutrality.

3

The Arbitrariness Argument

Hereafter *as such* is to be regarded neither less nor more than Now.

Sidgwick, *The Method of Ethics*

In Spring 2015, I spent a sabbatical in Singapore, a nation obsessed with planning. NTUC Income is a large investment firm on the island, and at the time they were running a campaign called "Future You." At bus stops, billboards, and movie theaters, they had posters and videos depicting a young professional (roughly my age) being greeted by his/her self from the future. In some of the ads, the future self warmly embraces the startled younger self. In others, the future self beats the younger counterpart. Each ad ends with "How will the Future You thank you?"[1] The implied message: open a retirement account with NTUC or fear the wrath of your future self.

It is no surprise that NTUC wants you to start an investment account—they'll make commissions right now on every stock you trade. Likewise, it is no surprise that the United States government has a vested interest in my making contributions to an individual retirement account—every contribution I make takes a bit of pressure off of the social security system, freeing up resources for other government projects. But we don't just think saving is good because it benefits banks or governments. (Very little of *my* altruism is directed at bankers and politicians.) The implied message of the NTUC ads is that it is in your *self*-interest to make these kinds of sacrifices. You are meant to see the ads and think: "That future person is just as much *me*. I should care about her as much as I care about myself now."

Is this good reasoning?

[1] See the "The Future Made Different" campaign. Designed for NTUC Income by Bartle Bogle Hagarty Global.

In this chapter and the next, we'll consider a second argument for future neutrality. This one is focused on the arbitrariness of privileging your present over your future. As with the last chapter, I will present the argument with some historical context and then consider some key objections.

3.1 The Arbitrariness Argument

The Epicureans thought that self-interest is only a matter of improving subjective experience—some event is only good for you if you experience it as pleasurable and only bad for you if you experience it as painful. The Epicureans thus famously thought that death could not be bad for you, since you won't have experiences when you die (an argument we'll return to in Chapter 7). In developing their view, the Epicureans encounter a problem related to the Life-Saving Argument—won't a person who only pursues pleasure end up having, on the whole, a less pleasurable life? Mindless hedonism is no way to happiness. The objection assumes that such a hedonist will only pursue *present* pleasures, and the Epicureans had a clever response. In his *Letter to Menoeceus*, Epicurus distinguishes the claim that every pleasure is good for a life—a view he endorses—from the claim that every pleasure should be chosen when offered—a view he rejects. Echoing Plato, he insists "it is right to judge all (pains and pleasures) by comparative measurement . . . For we sometimes treat the good as a bad, and conversely the bad as a good."[2] The Epicureans insisted we should learn not to discount potential pleasurable experiences just because of when they are scheduled.

The Epicurean concept of pleasure measurement was rehabilitated 1,600 years later by utilitarian philosopher Jeremy Bentham in his "hedonic calculus." Like the Epicureans, Bentham thought the basis for both self-interest and morality was reducible to two related dictums: maximize pleasure and minimize pain. In weighing potential pleasures and pains, Bentham introduced a series of variables that might serve as a basis for discounting. Certainty is one—we should prefer certain pleasures over riskier ones. Duration and intensity of the experiences should also be measured, taking account of diminishing marginal returns. Bentham also

[2] See Warren (2014: 176) for discussion.

allowed a fourth variable—"propinquity"—to be considered. Propinquity is the measure of how temporally remote an event is.[3] Why does remoteness count against a potential pleasure? Bentham gives us little by way of argument for this variable. His likely motivation was that remoteness often does play a role in our judgments of subjective value, so utilitarians should account for it.

Bentham built near bias into his hedonic calculus, but his fellow utilitarians quickly repudiated this, echoing Epicurus' point that there is something objectionably arbitrary about our focusing on the near pleasures. In Chapter 2 of *Utilitarianism*, John Stuart Mill calls near bias a common "infirmity of character." In commenting on Bentham's remoteness variable, Henry Sidgwick writes, "my feelings a year hence should be just as important to me as my feelings next minute, if only I could make an equally sure forecast of them."[4] Further on Sidgwick gives his argument for rejecting temporal discounting:

> The proposition 'that one ought to aim at one's own good' is sometimes given as the maxim of Rational Self-Love or Prudence . . . we might express it concisely by saying that 'Hereafter *as such* is to be regarded neither less nor more than Now.' It is not, of course, meant that the good of the present may not reasonably be preferred to that of the future on account of its greater certainty: or again, that a week ten years hence may not be more important to us than a week now, through an increase in our means or capacities of happiness. All that the principle affirms is that the mere difference of priority and posteriority in time is not a reasonable ground for having more regard for the consciousness of one moment than to that of another.[5]

He goes on to note that while the principle is most commonly invoked in hedonic tradeoffs, it need not be. It could be deployed for any theory of what constitutes your overall good.

We can make Sidgwick's points into a more succinct and precise argument:

The Arbitrariness Argument for Future Neutrality

(1) At any given time, a prudentially rational agent's preferences are insensitive to arbitrary differences. (The Non-Arbitrariness principle)

(2) Relative distance from the present is an arbitrary difference between events.

[3] See Chapter 4 of Bentham (1988).
[4] Sidgwick (1884: 120fn).
[5] Sidgwick (1884: 380–1).

(3) If you are near-biased, your preferences are sensitive to when an event is scheduled relative to the present.
C. So at any given time, near-biased preferences are not rationally permissible.

The Non-Arbitrariness principle in Premise (1) can range over a variety of relata: experiences, objects, persons, events, or possible worlds. And improper sensitivity can manifest in at least two ways. First, you might be sensitive to some feature that is completely irrelevant. Second, you might overestimate the relevance of a particular feature. In the case of Premise (2), we are to assume that you have already taken probability into account—you aren't using facts about scheduling merely as ways to approximate relative certainty. Premise (3) follows from how we have defined near bias, namely as having some future discount function.

The controversial premises are (1) and (especially) (2). In the rest of this chapter, I will develop the case for Premise (1), the Non-Arbitrariness principle. I'll consider what it takes for preferences to be objectionably arbitrary. In the next chapter we'll look in detail at Premise (2) and how future discounting relates to debates about personal identity over time.

3.2 Arbitrariness and Bias

Why believe Premise (1)? The best defense of the premise comes from consideration of cases: the Non-Arbitrariness principle offers the best explanation of why we judge a family of cases as paradigmatically irrational.[6] For instance, consider what's going wrong in the following thought experiment, originally offered by Derek Parfit:

> **Future Tuesdays:** A certain hedonist cares greatly about the quality of his future experiences. With one exception . . . he has *Future-Tuesday-Indifference*. Throughout every Tuesday he cares in the normal way about what is happening to him. But he never cares about possible pains or pleasures on a future Tuesday. Thus he would choose a painful operation on the following Tuesday rather than a much less painful operation on the following Wednesday. This choice would not be the result of any false beliefs. This man knows that the operation will be much more painful if it is on Tuesday. Nor does he have false beliefs

[6] These cases are also discussed in Finochiarro and Sullivan (2016).

about personal identity. He agrees that it will be just as much him who will be suffering on Tuesday. Nor does he have false beliefs about time. He knows that Tuesday is merely part of a conventional calendar, with an arbitrary name taken from a false religion. Nor has he any other beliefs that might help to justify his indifference to pain on future Tuesdays. This indifference is a bare fact. When he is planning his future, it is simply true that he always prefers the prospect of great suffering on a Tuesday to the mildest pain on any other day.[7]

Parfit judges this man to have irrational preferences. What explains their irrationality? The fact that his preferences vary *in arbitrary ways*. There is simply no reason to prefer some future pains over others merely because they fall on a particular day of the week. If the hedonist is indifferent between experiencing pain on Wednesdays and Thursdays, he should likewise be indifferent to whether his pain is scheduled for a Tuesday.

Future Tuesdays is a far-fetched case.[8] But the Non-Arbitrariness principle can also explain our reactions to much more common cases of criticizable bias. For example:

Detergents: Tim's local grocery store stocks three kinds of detergent: Wisk, Surf, and Tide. Each is composed of the same cleaning agents, and Tim is aware of this. Wisk and Surf are stocked on the same shelf at about waist height. Tide is one shelf above them at eye level. Tide is more expensive than either of the other brands.

Tim finds he is indifferent between Wisk and Surf, but he prefers Tide to either of the other detergents. In fact, he is willing to pay the difference to get Tide and regularly chooses that brand.

Tim's preferences are rationally criticizable. The only difference between any of the detergents is their location. Relative location is no reason, by itself, to discriminate between cleaning products. Given that there are no rationally significant differences, Tim ought to be indifferent between the detergents. Indeed, to the extent that he has reason to care about money, he should prefer the other detergents to Tide. And when we discover Tim's disposition to choose Tide (and know these background facts about the

[7] Parfit (1984: 123–4).

[8] Street (2009) considers whether Future Tuesdays gives us any evidence that we have attitude-independent reasons, and she argues that the esoteric nature of the case gives us reason to doubt its value.

case) we figure that he is biased—his preferences are not appropriately grounded in reasons.

The Non-Arbitrariness principle is also in the background of many discussions about cognitive biases. For example, consider the endowment effect, a bias in preferences identified by Daniel Kahneman, Jack Knetsch, and Richard Thaler in what has become one of the key studies in behavioral economics:

> **Mugs:** Subjects were divided into three groups: Buyers, Choosers, and Sellers. Buyers were offered the chance to buy a souvenir mug, and on average were willing to pay \$2.87. Choosers were given the choice of receiving a mug or some money, and on average they were indifferent between the mug and \$3.12. Sellers were given a mug and then asked how much they would sell it for, and on average they were indifferent between the mug and \$7.12.[9]

There is something criticizable about people who value a mug twice as much just because they have (very briefly) owned it. After all, they own their money as well. Why should the order in which the transactions happen matter? Kahneman, Knetsch, and Thaler explain the difference in terms of different attitudes we have towards goods that are classified as "for exchange"—like money—and goods that are classified as "for use"—like mugs. Owning a mug even briefly is enough to classify it as "for use" and therefore less fungible.

When we exhibit the endowment effect, framing effect, or any other of the myriad biases studied in behavioral economics, we are exhibiting irrationality. As Kahneman says in other work, "rational choices should satisfy some elementary requirement of consistency and coherence."[10] Non-Arbitrariness is among these elementary requirements. Why do we exhibit the endowment effect? Kahneman hypothesizes that our automatic evaluation system is evolutionarily wired to be sensitive to losses and to produce greater stress when an object previously owned and classified for use is taken away. We'll consider theories of error like this more directly in Chapter 8.

[9] Kahneman (2011: 295–6). See Kahneman et al. (1990) for the original studies demonstrating the endowment effect.

[10] Tversky and Kahneman (1981: 453).

3.3 Should We Be Permissive?

I think cases like Future Tuesdays, Detergents, and Mugs offer the best defense of the Non-Arbitrariness principle, since without some non-arbitrariness requirement, we have difficulty explaining why we find such preferences rationally questionable. There is another, more direct but more controversial route to defending the Non-Arbitrariness principle. We've been assuming that preferences are rational or irrational insofar as they are properly based on reasons. We might wonder: how tight is the connection between reasons and rational preferences? *Preference impermissivists* think the connection is *very* tight; your reasons determine exactly one set of rationally permissible preferences. Impermissivists endorse a uniqueness principle for rational preferences:

> **Preference Uniqueness:** Any total set of reasons at a time uniquely determines a set of rational preferences at a time.

Your set of total reasons include all of the facts you explicitly entertain when forming your preferences along with all of your background knowledge. We rarely share our total reasons with another person, but Uniqueness entails that if we do, rationality requires that our preferences be identical. If I am rational in preferring A to B, and we have the same total reasons, then the only rationally permissible preference for you is also preferring A to B. Likewise, if you have a total set of reasons at one time and form a rational preference based on those reasons, then the only way you can rationally change your preference is if your reasons somehow change. In contrast to the impermissivists, preference *permissivists* think there are at least some occasions where a total set of reasons justifies more than one set of preferences. They think you can sometimes rationally change your preferences without gaining or losing any evidence. And they think rational agents can sometimes have the same reasons but different preferences.

Why believe in Preference Uniqueness? It can explain our reaction to some otherwise hard-to-diagnose cases of objectionable preference formation.[11] For example:

[11] Based on parallel cases in the literature on belief and evidence inspired by White (2014). Chapter 8 of Hedden (2015b) also describes strong and weak preference uniqueness principles and defends them against permissivist counterexamples. Hedden's arguments assume that desires are beliefs about betterness, akin to the bridging principles we will discuss in the next section. I think we should reject such bridging principles. For other defenses of permissivism about belief, see Meacham (2013) and Kelly (2014).

Pills and Politics: In 2016 I have a set of reasons that bear on the question of who I hope wins the democratic primary: Bernie Sanders or Hillary Clinton. Suppose the total set of reasons is permissive—it supports preferring that either candidate win or being indifferent. Suppose also that I can form my electoral preference in one of two ways. Option 1: I can carefully delineate my reasons and form a preference on that basis. Option 2: I can take one of two pills: a "Bernie pill," which induces a preference for a Sanders victory, or a "Hillary pill," which induces a preference for a Clinton victory. Suppose I am short on time and opt for the pill route. I take a Bernie pill, becoming a passionate advocate of his candidacy. I get into arguments with my Clinton-supporting friends about their hopes for America. And I engage in the other sorts of activities you might expect of a partisan political agent. Should I think my partisanship is rational? And if I accidentally ingest a Hillary pill later, should I then be relieved I didn't vote for Bernie?

The permissivist seems committed to thinking I am rational in my partisanship. My actions and judgments are based on rational preferences, after all. But once I realize that I could have just as easily popped a Hillary pill, shouldn't that give me pause in my committed campaigning? It seems that permissivists also have a problem explaining the value we place on the methods we use to form our preferences. Preference impermissivism doesn't have the problem of explaining what's wrong with pill-based politicking. A pill-based method has no guarantee of leading to the uniquely correct preferences, so it is a poor method for forming rational preferences.

Preference impermissivism entails the Non-Arbitrariness principle. To see why, assume the Non-Arbitrariness principle is false—assume that it is sometimes rationally permissible for preferences to vary based on arbitrary differences. We can define an arbitrary difference as any fact (or purported fact) that lacks normative significance, and therefore cannot be included in a total set of reasons for an agent at a time. If the Non-Arbitrariness principle is false, then it is possible for two agents to have different, rationally permissible preferences based on the exact same total set of reasons R, because it is rationally permissible for either of the agents to have preferences sensitive to facts not included in their total set of reasons R. But the Uniqueness principle says this is impossible. So the Uniqueness principle entails the Non-Arbitrariness principle.

The Non-Arbitrariness principle does not, however, entail the Uniqueness principle. It is perfectly coherent to hold that rational preferences are insensitive to arbitrary differences, but that total sets of reasons fail to determine a unique set of rationally permissible preferences. Suppose the only reasons that two agents have for backing their political preferences come from facts about the domestic economy. Permissivists might hold that such facts are normatively significant but they back either supporting Sanders or supporting Clinton or being indifferent between the two. In this case, preferences satisfy the Non-Arbitrariness principle but not the Uniqueness principle.

I ultimately find the Uniqueness principle unappealing, because it rules out any possibility of faultless preference change—rationally permissible preference change without any change in underlying reasons. Indeed, preference permissivism helps us better understand why it has been so hard to distinguish rational and irrational preference change over time. For instance, I assume that while our emotions sometimes provide reasons for our preferences, they do not always provide reasons. I might be aware of all of the reasons that I need to have a root canal and prefer (on the basis of these reasons) to schedule the procedure for next week. I can anticipate in advance that I'll be nervous before the procedure. Sure enough, on the day of the procedure, none of these reasons have changed, but I now feel the anxiety. This does not give me any *new* reason to delay the procedure, though the experience of the anxiety might sway me to prefer delaying the procedure. As a matter of course, the activation of our time-biased emotions often affects our preferences. But if impermissivism were true, then any such preference change would be automatically irrational. And as a consequence, it would be too easy to argue that our time-biased preferences are irrational. So in assuming permissivism, I will make the case harder for the critic of time bias. We'll talk about this issue in some detail in Chapters 6 and 8. But for now, note simply that for those tempted to endorse preference impermissivism, there is another good reason to endorse the Non-Arbitrariness requirement.

3.4 Problems for Non-Arbitrariness?

Premise (1) of the Arbitrariness Argument is motivated by the view that preferences are irrational if they are not properly backed by reasons. On such a view, we can understand an irrational bias as a preference that is not backed by reasons, or a preference whose strength does not accurately reflect the weights, permissions, and requirements offered by those reasons.[12]

Will such a requirement be too strong? You might worry that such a requirement would lead us to declare certain preferences irrational which seem perfectly rationally permissible. Here is a case that seems to challenge the Non-Arbitrariness principle:

Cookies: I prefer chocolate cookies to peanut butter cookies.

At first glance, it might seem there are no reasons underwriting a preference for one type of cookie over another. So this preference is not rationally permissible by the lights of the Non-Arbitrariness principle.

But push a bit further and some candidates for normatively significant facts suggest themselves. I might be wired in such a way as to experience more pleasure from chocolate than peanut butter. Or I might have meaningful associations with chocolate cookies—perhaps because we have traditionally eaten them as a treat in my family. These facts are normatively significant with an appropriately lenient view of what can count as a reason.[13] In fact, it would be an odd situation wherein, after some reflection, I couldn't come up with *any* reasons for my cookie preference. And in such a case, it seems less odd to classify my preference as an irrational chocolate bias. This strategy can be generalized to preferences for people, events, or experiences. For instance, while it might seem arbitrary that you prefer to marry one identical twin over his brother, it is easy enough to cite a history of shared experiences with one as the reason-giving feature of your preference.

Will adhering to the Non-Arbitrariness principle ever lead you to be worse off than an agent who forms arbitrary preferences? It would be troubling if there were many cases where the Non-Arbitrariness principle conflicts with the Success principle motivated in Chapter 2. Consider another culinary example that suggests a tension:

Dates: You are offered a choice of two identical dates to eat. One is to your right and the other is to your left. You want a date, but you can only eat one. You find you prefer the date on the right, and you choose to eat it.

[12] Determining the weights of reasons is a significant puzzle in contemporary normative theory. For an overview of the issues, see Lord and Maguire (2016).

[13] Indeed, there is a lot of evidence that there are weighty reasons underwriting many of our food preferences. See Wilson (2015).

The dates case comes from twelfth-century philosopher Abu Hamid al-Ghazali, and is a key example in the long tradition of debates about whether undetermined choices are rational (a theme in the philosophical literature on free will).[14] The Non-Arbitrariness requirement entails that a preference for the date to the right is irrational since being to the right and being to the left are not normatively significant properties. Is it wrong to criticize a preference for the right date?

In considering this case we should draw a distinction between rationally criticizable *preferences* and rationally criticizable *actions*. It may well be that you can act correctly even though your preferences and intentions with respect to the specific goods on offer are irrational. This is a common lesson from so-called "Buridan's ass" cases. You need to form an intention that favors one of your options over others in order to act. You ought to act (at the risk of missing out on a good). But whatever intention you form is criticizable because it is not based on a reason. The Non-Arbitrariness principle does not entail that you are irrational to choose whatever date you in fact choose. It only insists that if your *preferences* discriminate among the dates, you must have some reason for the discrimination. Compare this to a case where you find you prefer the right date to the left, are offered the left, but are also offered the chance to pay some sum (however small) to switch. We'd criticize you for paying to realize this preference, since there is simply no reason to pay more for a duplicate fruit. If the only differences between the options are arbitrary, you should prefer merely to have some date or other. And you should realize that preference in your actions by picking one of the dates. Once we appropriately distinguish rational preferences and rational actions, such cases do not create a tension between the Non-Arbitrariness and Success principles.

Will adhering to the Non-Arbitrariness principle lead to a vicious regress of reasons and preferences?[15] Suppose Connor prefers washing his clothes with detergent rather than washing his clothes with toilet water. If his preference is rational, it is appropriately backed by reasons. The fact that detergent cleans clothes serves as one reason to back his preference. But you might wonder whether Connor's total set of reasons also needs to include a further fact, namely that Connor prefers his clothes be clean. After all, if he doesn't mind smelling like the loo, why bother

[14] Kane (2005: 37).

[15] Thanks to Richard Fumerton for discussion of this objection.

with detergent? We might call such preferences *bridging preferences*, since they make facts about the world (i.e., detergents clean things) relevant to agents' preferences (i.e., Connor prefers detergent). Do the reasons that back a preference always require such bridging preferences? If so, then it seems the Non-Arbitrariness requirement leads to a vicious regress, since each bridging preference will also require reasons, which will require further bridging preferences, which will demand further reasons . . . it won't end. But without bridging preferences, the objection goes, it is hard to see how facts about the world could be relevant to self-interest.

To block the regress, we should reject the assumption that reasons backing a preference must include a bridging preference. The fact that detergent cleans clothes is a reason for Connor to prefer detergent to toilet water even if he hasn't formed an attitude about whether he prefers his clothes be clean. As long as clean clothes are in his self-interest, this is enough for the detergent fact to feature as a reason for Connor. More broadly, I do not think our reasons to have certain preferences are always based in further preferences any more than our reasons to act are always based in our desires. To avoid the regress, I take it as primitive whether some fact is normatively significant for some agent's preferences. I endorse a version of *externalism* about prudential reasons. And in this spirit, I assume that the reasons that can satisfy the Non-Arbitrariness requirement may nevertheless sometimes fail to motivate agents to adopt certain preferences or perform certain actions.

Could you have explicit reasons to be near-biased, ones that would make future discounting non-arbitrary? If so, it seems the Arbitrariness Argument could be circumvented.[16] Suppose you admire James Dean and his impulsive "you only live once" attitude. Being cool like Dean seems to require discounting the future. For a certain class of agents, such reasons of coolness might provide independent grounds for future discounting (especially if they are unmoved by the Success arguments from the previous chapter).

Of course most of us do not have such reasons, and so this is not a psychologically realistic option for us to avoid the Arbitrariness Argument. Further, it is somewhat puzzling to understand how you would engage in the Dean-inspired reasoning about your preferences. For instance, it

[16] Thanks to Tom Dougherty for discussion here.

is not as though a desire for coolness could lead you to endorse a policy of cultivating impulsivity—such a policy would be self-defeating. More likely, you find yourself with the personality trait of impulsivity, and you value that trait now in such a way that gives you reason now to discount. But in this case, you don't have a stable near bias. Rather you are biased towards the option that seems coolest.

A final and more serious worry about the Non-Arbitrariness principle is that it threatens to overgeneralize, wiping out any distinction between prudence and altruism. Some philosophers have thought that the Arbitrariness Argument for Future Neutrality also requires *agent* neutrality—the view that rationality requires indifference as to who is benefited or harmed from a given event.[17] For example, Derek Parfit uses considerations about arbitrariness to argue that self-interest is incoherent:

> I suggest that the principle of self-interest has no force. There are only two genuine competitors in this particular field. One is the principle of biased rationality: do what will best achieve what you actually want. The other is the principle of impartiality: do what is in the best interests of everyone concerned. The apparent force of the principle of self-interest derives, I think, from these other two principles.... Suppose a man does not care what happens to him in, say, the more distant future. To such a man, the principle of self-interest can only be propped up by an appeal to the principle of impartiality. We must say, 'Even if you don't care, you ought to take what happens to you then equally into account.' But for this, as a special claim, there seem to me no good arguments. It can be supported as part of the general claim, 'You ought to take what happens to everyone equally into account.'[18]

Parfit argues further that once the temporal intervals get sufficiently long (and personal changes sufficiently dramatic), saving for oneself is not normatively different from giving to another.

Parfit goes too far. We can distinguish between sacrifices made for one's own future and sacrifices made for others in a non-arbitrary way. The key difference is that you are eventually *compensated* for your self-interested future sacrifices, but you are not necessarily compensated for

[17] Thomas Nagel famously relies on the apparent parity of the considerations for temporal neutrality and agent neutrality to argue against the rationality of agent-relative bias (Nagel 1970b).

[18] Parfit (1971: 26).

the sacrifices you make on behalf of others.[19] The fact that you (rather than someone else) will be the beneficiary of the sacrifice is a non-arbitrary basis for the preference. In this spirit, David Brink argues that the crucial difference between sacrificing for your future self and sacrificing for others is that your life composes an organic whole, while groups of people do not.[20] He goes on to argue that we couldn't be rational planning agents unless we thought of ourselves as such unities.[21]

There is a significant difference between rational prudence and rational altruism, and Brink is right to look to facts about compensation as the source of this distinction. But his defense of prudence depends on this assumption that we are organic unities and rationally view ourselves as such. Are Sidgwick, Brink, and others right that the only differences between our present and our future are arbitrary? What motivates Premise (2) of the Arbitrariness Argument? These questions draw us into some longstanding philosophical debates about personal identity and egoistic concern—debates that form the subject of the next chapter.

[19] Brink (2010: 360–6). Whiting (1986) attributes the compensation argument to Butler and Sidgwick.

[20] Brink (2003: 224).

[21] A point that is also developed in much greater detail in Korsgaard (2009).

4

Personal Volatility

> The most important difference between human beings and beasts is this: Beasts, insofar as they are moved by sense, conciliate themselves only to what is at hand and present, since they are aware of very little of the past and future. A human being, on the other hand, shares in reasons, through which he traces consequences, sees the causes of things, notices the mutual relations of effects and causes, compares similarities, and combines and connects future with present things, and so he easily sees the course of his whole life, and prepares the things necessary for living that life.
>
> Cicero, *On Obligations*[1]

As we've seen in earlier chapters, prudentially rational agents pay attention to the potential for change. For instance, suppose I am comparing potential retirement investments in the US bond market and Greek bond market. I should be a lot less confident that I know what will happen to money put in the Greek bonds since their economy is more likely to change in unpredictable ways. The Greeks need to sweeten the deal for potential investors, selling their bonds at a low price now to compensate for the risk. Let's call the range of probabilities assigned to potential outcomes of a choice the choice's *outcome volatility*. The wider the range of potential outcomes and probabilities, the more volatile the choice. And when you discount the present value of an option based on its probability of occurring, we've called this *probabilistic discounting*. Rationality requires you to take outcome volatility into account, though of course the probabilities are not always easy to judge. Much work in decision theory aims to offer an account of how rational agents should act given their approximations of outcome volatility.

But what if you also think that *you* are volatile over long intervals of time? Do facts about how you will change over time provide reasons to

[1] Translation from Irwin (2007: 312).

discount your interests in the distant future? That is the subject of this chapter. (And later, Chapter 10)

Let's call the range of your variation over time your *personal volatility*. For example, for most normally developing adolescents, the interval from ages ten to nineteen is highly personally volatile. Your body grows, becoming significantly hairier and smellier. Your brain undergoes synaptic pruning. Your personality (hopefully) matures. The shorter interval from age nineteen to twenty is significantly less volatile. When you discount the present value of an option because of changes you predict you will undergo before the scheduled outcome is realized, we can call this *personal discounting*.

Personal discounting and probabilistic discounting can also come apart, as my India splurge in Chapter 1 illustrates. I am confident enough in the probabilities on each of my two options (spend or save). I just don't now care much about myself so far out, since I predict that I will change so much. This indicates another key difference between the forms of volatility. Outcome volatility is measured using the probabilities of different future events occurring, where those events can be described aperspectivally (i.e., suppose there is an 80% chance of my stocks appreciating, then the problem can be posed as there is an 80% chance that Sullivan will withdraw $24,000 in 2040 and a 20% chance she will not—which world is preferable?). But the question of personal volatility only arises from the first-personal, temporally situated point of view (i.e., does Sullivan in 2040 matter enough *to me, now,* in a self-interested way?).

Personal discounting can be modeled with a discount function, like other forms of future discounting we've surveyed. For instance, it may be that even if I have a steep personal discount function, I would still be willing to contribute to a retirement scheme if the potential payoff were large enough. I might be unwilling to save $3,000 now for a $24,000 retirement payout if I think I will change significantly in the interim. But the prospect of converting $3,000 to $1M in thirty-one years might be enough to tempt me even after weighing my volatility.

4.1 Single-Self and Multiple-Self Models

Even raising the question of personal discounting requires wading into a debate about the metaphysical and psychological indispensability of subjectivity. *Whole-hearted reductionists* about personal identity believe (1) that the facts about a person's identity over time just consist in the holding of certain particular facts that can be described entirely without reference to a subject, and (2) that these impersonal facts are the only facts that are relevant to rational planning.[2] In contrast, *non-reductionists* deny both (1) and (2). And *half-hearted reductionists* think subjectivity could be eliminated from the complete metaphysical description of the world, but they think subjectivity is an ineliminable part of rational planning.[3]

Whole-hearted reductionists have no special concern for personal volatility. If Parfit is taken at his word, he was once a whole-hearted reductionist. "I find (reductionism) liberating, and consoling. When I believed that my existence was a further fact, I seemed imprisoned in myself. My life seemed like a glass tunnel, through which I was moving faster every year, and at the end of which there was darkness. When I changed my view, the walls of my glass tunnel disappeared."[4] But few of us are capable of sustaining this attitude, at least psychologically. Parfit himself eventually lost heart and denied whole-hearted reductionism.[5]

Nor is it obvious what it would be to adopt such a detached view of our lives. Even if sometimes you can imaginatively "step outside" yourself and consider your life as a connected stream of stages, the bird's eye perspective on your life is still *a perspective*, imagined from its own apparently personal, present vantage. Much of the literature on personal identity presupposes that we have secure intuitions about what rationally matters to us (or would matter in a counterfactual scenario). Popular theories use these intuitions as evidence for various theories of what it is to be a persisting self or, at least, what we take ourselves to be. For instance, David Velleman sets out to argue that we care most about occupying selves with perspectives (rather than strict numerical persistence). He argues for this using data about concern: "What we most want to know about our survival . . . is how much of the future we are in a position to anticipate experiencing. We peer up the stream of consciousness, so to speak, and wonder how far up there is still a stream to see . . . My question is how long there will be someone to occupy the position that is the center of my self-centered projections."[6] On a different track, Jennifer Whiting thinks our patterns of actual or counterfactual rational egoistic concern

[2] For instance, Parfit (1984).

[3] For instance, Lewis (1979) or Paul (2014). For more on this as a metaphysical view, see Section 3 of Zimmerman (2005).

[4] Parfit (1984: 281).

[5] Parfit (1999).

[6] Velleman (1996: 67–8).

give evidence that we are most concerned with which future or past selves we can bear an analogue of the friendship relationship towards.[7] David Lewis thinks that because both survival and psychological connectedness matter for rational egoistic concern, we should think of ourselves as four-dimensional perdurants.[8]

I confess, I find this direction of argument puzzling. Velleman and Whiting, for instance, ask us to imagine reality as though it is a field of candidate selves, and we need to figure out which of these selves we could occupy or befriend. But I already had a very strong pre-philosophical understanding of what it is to be myself, even if that understanding eludes metaphysical specification. I believe I've persisted for thirty-four years, that I have many properties, which now give me reason to plan for the future in certain ways, and that I also have some biases, which sometimes prevent me from properly attending to my reasons. My more pressing philosophical concern is to figure out what I should care about. I am much more likely to revise any of my views about rational egoistic concern than I am to revise my self-conception.

Indeed, we should be cautious about how we state the planning problems to begin with. As we've seen in other cases in this book (most notably the Future You ad campaign), there is a tendency to describe planning problems as involving coordination between multiple selves.[9] There are two features of the multiple-self model worth making explicit. First, on the model, reasoning and planning are done by your short-lived present self on behalf of many distinct, also short-lived future selves. Why are those selves important to you now? On the multiple-self theory, it is because they have some special relation to the present self, and that relation is the basis of egoistic concern. Second, the view fits most naturally with a stage theory of personal persistence. According to the stage theory, ordinary objects and persons just are short-lived stages. Stages compose longer-lived objects, for instance the object that is your lifespan. But we most identify with particular stages at a time.[10] According to the stage view, individual stages have temporal properties

[7] Whiting (1986). [8] Lewis (1976).

[9] This approach goes back at least to Plato's *Symposium*; see Irwin (2007: 110). Locke popularized it in Book II, Chapter XXVII of his *Essay Concerning Human Understanding*, see Locke (1975). And Parfit made this model dominant in the contemporary personal identity literature.

[10] Sider (1996).

like *having been a child* in virtue of being appropriately related to other stages which have those properties.

We can contrast the multiple-self model with the *single-self model.* On the single-self model, when you plan your future, you are planning for events that will happen to you—your present self—a self who will also exist at some later time. On this model, you view yourself as an enduring object, an object that is "wholly" present at every moment of its life and doesn't persist through time and change by having distinctly existing stages.

With a few qualifications, we can translate between the two models when it comes to describing planning puzzles. On the single-self model, we ask whether I will benefit from some present sacrifice. But on the multiple-self model, we ask whether my present self should make some sacrifice for a future self. On the multiple-self model, egoistic concern is determined by how my present self is related to some future self (treated as a distinct entity in the model). But on the single-self model, egoistic concern is a matter of asking what I will be like at a future time and whether, in the interim, something will happen that causes me to care less about what happens to me then.

Here are the three qualifications. First, multiple-self models require more assumptions to explain how facts about core identities can figure in rational planning. We often plan, act, and form preferences based on our beliefs about our core identities.[11] Consider a case:

> **Monet:** It is 1865 and Claude Monet is deliberating about whether it is worth it to finish *The Woman in the Green Dress*. He has no reason to think finishing the painting will bring happiness or accolades—indeed, most of his work is ignored or derided by French critics. But he reasons that because he is an artist, he prefers the work be finished. Being an artist means having certain aspirations for one's works.

I prefer this book be published because I'm a philosopher, and being a philosopher is a reason to write philosophical books. Alan prefers he finish the race because he is a marathoner. Identity facts like these ought to be admissible as reasons for the preferences we have.

[11] This point has been made by psychologists like Duckworth (2016: Chapter 12). And it is also pressed by philosophers like Wolf (1986) and Korsgaard (2009: 21–4).

On the multiple-self model, if you are going to appeal to a fact about what or who you are, then you need an account of how that kind of fact could apply to the short-lived stage doing the planning. More precisely, advocates of the multiple-self model are forced to make one of three claims about core identities:

Option 1. Core identity properties are intrinsic to their bearer, and something can have such properties even if it has a very brief existence.

Option 2. Core identity properties are always extrinsic to their bearer, and whether an individual self has such properties always depends in some way on the activities of other selves (namely, her other selves at other times).

Option 3. There are no core identity properties, and so such properties never provide reasons for planning.

Option 1 seems implausible as a theory of what it is to be a philosopher, artist, or marathoner; you must have a history in order to exemplify such properties. Nothing comes into existence ex nihilo with a core identity. Likewise, Option 3 seems to force the multiple-self theorist into a radically impoverished theory of rational planning. Option 2 seems the most promising, but on this model, it is incorrect to say that your core identity is what characterizes the present, planning agent. It might be that core identities only apply to whole collections of stages in a life of which you (the short-lived self) are a small part. In this case, unless this collection of stages has the ability to think and plan, no present thinker or planner has such an identity. Or it might be that your present stage indirectly inherits this property from the collection of which it is a part. But then you might think this fails to be a genuine identity property, since it is only held indirectly. The single-self model, in contrast, has no special issue of how a self inherits and maintains core identity properties. One and the same self can have existed long enough and acquired the right kind of history to be an artist, philosopher, or marathoner *now*.

Here is a second qualification. Describing planning problems in terms of multiple selves can obscure data about egoistic concern. Strong indexical words like "I" have special cognitive significance that non-indexical descriptions like "a 2048 self" do not. In particular, strongly indexical beliefs have more *motivational* force than their non-indexical counterparts. Consider a famous thought experiment from John Perry:

> **The Careless Shopper:** John believes that the shopper with a torn sugar sack is making a mess. But he does not rearrange his cart—he just keeps walking around the store, trying unsuccessfully to catch up with the careless shopper. Then he makes the sudden realization that he is the shopper with a torn sack. And so he acquires a new belief, as he puts it: "*I* am making a mess."[12]

John might not be particularly concerned to check his cart until he forms the belief that "*I* am making a mess." There is a longstanding debate in the philosophy of language as to whether words like "I" can have the same meaning as more impersonal descriptions (i.e., "Meghan Sullivan at 2017" or "the author of this book"). Even without wading too deep into these semantic questions, we can acknowledge that the first-personal descriptions tend to be more motivationally significant than similar third-personal descriptions. And when we are engaged in rational planning, the ways we describe a planning problem might matter quite a bit for our emotional response to our reasons. To the extent that we need to be motivated to appreciate our prudential reasons, we should favor strong indexicals like "I" when describing our future options rather than more impersonal expressions like "a future self."

Finally, there remains a lingering metaphysical question of what exactly "I" refers to. Perhaps our ordinary language is misleading, and all we really are are temporary selves planning for selves at other times. If this is the case, the extra motivational oomph of describing your future using first-personal vocabulary would also be misguided. (Indeed, this metaphysical picture can provide an argument for whole-hearted reductionism.) This brings me to my third and final reservation about unreflectively relying on multiple-self models. I do not think the stage theory is the right theory of how we persist through time. To lay my cards on the table, I am an endurantist—elsewhere I have developed the thesis that everything that undergoes change "wholly persists" through that change.[13] I do not think individual persons—or anything for that matter—are collections of multiple distinct stages spread out in time. So I think the single-self model

[12] Perry (1979). [13] Sullivan (2012a).

better lines up with the facts about our persistence conditions. Laying out my motivations for endurantism would take us too far afield of the current project. For now, note just that there is a major controversy in metaphysics over how things persist, and you should investigate these issues for yourself before taking multiple-self talk literally.

With these caveats and translation issues in mind, I'll still tend to switch between the models, especially since many of the views I will criticize are described in multiple-self terms.

4.2 Two Routes to Personal Discounting

Let's get back to the main argument: this chapter is aimed at the half-hearted reductionists and non-reductionists. If you acknowledge a first-personal perspective, either in reality or as an ineliminable part of your psychology and planning, then is personal discounting ever rational? If so, then rational personal discounting could license near bias. At least, it could block Premise (2) of the Arbitrariness Argument whenever volatile agents are reasoning about distant tradeoffs—the cases of near bias we most worry about. I will make the case that personal discounting is just one of our many psychological biases that prevent us from living prudently, much like our inability to properly estimate future values and our inability to control our strongly near-biased emotions. The recent philosophical literature on personal identity focuses on questions like what is it to be a persisting self, asking us to imagine changes and form judgments about whether we'd survive or still exhibit self-concern after those changes. Instead, I am going to assume that you already know (more or less) that you are some kind of persisting self capable of enduring somehow through change. I will ask what patterns of self-concern you ought to have, given what you think you are.

We will consider two strategies for defending personal discounting over long intervals of time. The first strategy focuses on qualitative personal volatility. Most of us will change significantly with respect to *how* we are over long intervals. Our personalities, quasi-memories, and aspirations will change.[14] Our bodies will change with respect to our

[14] A quasi-memory is a memory-like mental state that does not presuppose facts about persistence through time.

physical abilities, our features, and many of our parts. If similarity of qualitative properties is what matters for self-interest, then qualitative volatility would be a good basis for personal discounting.

The second strategy focuses on numerical personal volatility. Over long intervals, are we likely to change with respect to *how much* we are? And would this be a ground for thinking we are less of ourselves after change? If self-interest depends on facts about persistence and you are less and less you in the more distant future, then such numerical volatility would be a good basis for personal discounting. I will also consider whether there are possible metaphysical changes (i.e., fission) that could provide a rational basis for personal *mark-ups*—increases in future-directed egoistic concern.

I'll aim to convince you that, despite their initial appearances and auspicious philosophical lineages, these two strategies for defending personal discounting fail. The philosophical literature on egoistic concern is typically dominated by thought experiments involving teletransportation, brain dissection, and amnesia. But in line with a theme of this book, I'll lean towards a different methodology, drawing more on thought experiments from more realistic cases of volatility and empirical work on egoistic concern. The stakes are significant. Most of us are not doing nearly enough to plan for our distant future, and it is not usually because we have grim predictions about what we are, how long we will live, or what will happen to the world economy. More likely, it is because we are in the grip of biases in our egoistic concern.

4.3 A Qualitative Basis for Egoistic Concern?

Recall the Future You ads from the previous chapter. What is it about that pensioner in the ad that should make him/her matter to you in a self-interested way, rather than, say, in the more broadly moral way we care that the elderly have adequate financial resources? (We will assume for the foregoing arguments that there is a difference between caring self-interestedly and caring morally.) One flat-footed answer is that you just care that the future person will be *identical to you now*. But there are some puzzles for thinking mere identity is the basis of egoistic concern. Consider an example from Thomas Nagel. Suppose it turns out that people just are their bodies. When you die, you will permanently become a corpse. Would the discovery that you'll continue to exist as a corpse affect your rational planning? Probably not. That hunk of flesh embalmed in formaldehyde and buried in the ground some hundred years from now might be you, but you will care a lot less (if at all) about yourself *then*. Barring special religious reasons or moral concern for those we leave behind, most of us are unconcerned for our future corpses.[15] Thought experiments like this lend support to the view that our grounds for egoistic concern are something more substantive than just mere facts about identity. Though admittedly it is hard to conceive of how you could plan for an inanimate corpse even if you thought it had the basis of egoistic concern. We lack a theory of corpse well-being.

A variety of candidates have been advanced as the "missing ingredient" that we care about when we care self-interestedly. One of the most prominent views (suggested by John Locke and advanced especially by Derek Parfit) is that the basis for egoistic concern is psychological connectedness. Indeed, Parfit famously holds that strict identity doesn't matter at all, once we realize that connectedness is what matters.[16] Direct psychological connections come in two varieties. One variety of connection is similarity: you share the same memories, personality traits, preferences, and beliefs.[17] Another variety of connection is causal: your choices at a time cause your future memories, and your intentions at a time cause your future satisfaction or frustration. For most normally developing individuals, psychological connectedness comes in degrees. I am much more connected with the woman I was a year ago or will be a year hence than I am with my teenage self (who hated philosophy) or with my elder self (who will love slow river cruises). Psychological connectedness is also an intransitive relation, which explains why we might exhibit personal volatility over long intervals even if every stage of our life is strongly directly connected to its immediately antecedent and subsequent stages.

Within psychological connectedness theories there is also significant debate about whether the basis of egoistic concern must hold one–one

[15] Nagel (1970a).

[16] "Connectedness is a more important element in survival . . . Even if connectedness is not more important than continuity, the fact that one of these is a relation of degree is enough to show what matters in survival can have degrees" (Parfit 1971: 21).

[17] Defenders of the view often insist on similarity of "quasi-memories"—memory-like mental states that do not presuppose you are identical with your past self. This distinction does not matter for our purposes.

or could hold one–many. For instance, if you were scheduled to undergo fission in the near future, with the process resulting in two distinct selves with psychologies very strongly connected to yours now, would you care self-interestedly and equally about the fates of each of your daughter selves? Or are we only able to care self-interestedly about at most one future self at a time? And which of your duplicates should get access to your retirement fund? Parfit denies that strict identity is a basis of egoistic concern because he takes seriously the possibility of this type of numerical volatility. We will return to this issue in Section 4.7.

4.4 The Concern Argument

All but the most boring of us exhibit qualitative personal volatility. Our apparent memories fade, our personalities morph, our projects and intentions change directions. This suggests a general argument for why personal discounting is typically permissible over long intervals, one based on the nature of egoistic concern:

The Concern Argument for Personal Discounting

(1) There is some criterion C (like psychological connectedness) that determines your egoistic concern, and it comes in degrees.
(2) It is prudentially rational to discount events based on the degree to which those events have the basis for your egoistic concern.
(3) Given that you are a normally developing agent, as events are scheduled in the far future, C will tend to hold to a lesser and lesser degree. (The Qualitative Volatility Assumption)
C. As events are scheduled in the far future, it is rational to discount them.

Note the argument doesn't work if psychological continuity—a transitive relation—is the basis of egoistic concern. You are psychologically continuous with any future self that is connected to your present self via a series of unbroken relations of psychological connectedness. Psychological continuity isn't volatile the way connectedness is likely to be. Premise (2) seems to follow from the assumption that prudential rationality is a matter of self-interest—if an event has less of whatever matters to self-interest, it is perfectly rational to care less about it. But, as stated, the premise is ambiguous between what actually describes your pattern of egoistic concern and what you take to be a reason-giving basis for your egoistic concern. Premise (2) is only true on the second reading. So we should make the argument more precise by clarifying the first two premises:

The Concern Argument for Personal Discounting—Revised

(1*) There is some criterion C (like psychological connectedness) that determines your *rational* egoistic concern, and it comes in degrees.
(2*) It is prudentially rational to discount events based on the degree to which those events have C.
(3) Given that you are a normally developing agent, as events are scheduled in the far future, C will tend to hold to a lesser and lesser degree. (The Qualitative Volatility Assumption)
C. As events are scheduled in the far future, it is prudentially rational to discount them.

The Concern Argument, as stated, is highly general. It accommodates the prevailing philosophical view that self-interest is a matter of psychological connectedness. But it could equally work for some other theories of egoistic concern. For instance, if you think preservation of your body or your brain is what you really care about, then a bodily-connectedness or neuro-connectedness criterion of egoistic concern could be plugged into the argument. For instance, Jeff McMahan offers a version of the Concern Argument to justify caring less about yourself in the more distant future, and he thinks the basis of egoistic concern is a combination of psychological and neurological factors. According to McMahan, we minimally care about having our consciousness connected over time (and he assumes consciousness is realized in the brain). After we've satisfied ourselves that some future self's consciousness will be the same as ours, *then* we look to see how psychologically connected they are to us. We care more or less self-interestedly about that future self to the extent that they are more or less psychologically connected with us.[18]

4.5 Simple Connectedness and Moral Valence

The Concern Argument might seem initially appealing, but it is unsound. In this section, I will offer arguments against premise (1*), at least insofar

[18] McMahan (2002: 79–80).

as it purports to represent our actual judgments about egoistic concern. And I will argue that attempts to make premise (1*) psychologically realistic will undermine premise (3). We'll use as our case study the hypothesis that psychological connectedness is the basis for discounting. Then I will generalize the objections to other candidates for C.

Premise (1*) of the Concern Argument can be understood in two ways. First, it might be thought to make both a psychological prediction and a normative judgment. That is, C predicts our pattern of egoistic concern and that pattern is rational. Call this the *psychological reading*. Second, it might be thought to be only a revisionary normative judgment. That is, you might not in fact care at all about C but you rationally should. Call this the *revolutionary reading*. The Concern Argument looks significantly more plausible if premise (1*) is given the first reading. On the revolutionary reading, we need (at least) an independent argument for why C matters as well as a theory of error for why you are so ignorant of your self-interest.[19]

On the psychological reading, premise (1*) makes a prediction which is empirically testable, namely:

> **The Simple Connectedness Hypothesis:** We will have diminished egoistic concern for any selves who are psychologically dissimilar or causally disconnected from our present self.

But there are problem cases for this as a hypothesis about our actual patterns of concern. Consider the true story of Susannah Cahalan's brain disorder:

> **Brain on Fire:** In 2009, Susannah Cahalan had a sudden, radical mental breakdown. Until that point she was a healthy twenty-four-year-old living in New York and reporting for a major newspaper. She awoke one morning in the midst of a grand mal seizure. After that event, she lost her memory, experienced extreme paranoia and psychosis, and soon after, lost most of her emotional responses. After a month of living in this radically debilitating state, a doctor successfully diagnosed Cahalan with a rare form of encephalitis. The key to the diagnosis came when Cahalan was asked to draw and number a clock face. She drew a normal circle, but bunched all of the hours to the right-hand side—a

[19] Thanks to Johann Frick and Trenton Merricks for discussion here. See Chapter 1 of Merricks (2022) for an updated approach to identity and egoistic concern.

> common symptom of inflammation in the right side of the brain. After a course of treatment for encephalitis, Cahalan mostly returned to her pre-disease psychological functioning. She remembers life before the disease, but had to piece together life during her "month of madness" by watching hospital security footage and interviewing her caretakers.[20]

During her illness, Cahalan was not able to form new memories or preserve the old dimensions of her personality. The Simple Connectedness Hypothesis predicts that Cahalan should feel like a "new woman" after her recovery, not identifying in any significant way with her hospitalized self and troubled by the long disruption in the psychological connections with her previous self. It also predicts that she should have significantly diminished concern for what happened in her life during the period of the disease. In fact, neither of these hypotheses are true. Cahalan sees herself as having *recovered* from her disease, carrying on a life that now includes this horrific adventure as an episode. And she cared deeply enough about her life during the disease to watch tapes and conduct interviews, trying to understand what it was like for her when she was ill.

Of course, Cahalan is a reporter. Her concern can be explained in part by her desire to tell an interesting story. But that won't explain all of her interest (after all, she is not particularly concerned about other women's rare brain diseases). The more important question is whether Cahalan's egoistic concern depends on her psychological connectedness (as the Simple Connectedness Hypothesis predicts) or whether her interest in establishing psychological connectedness is driven by pre-existing egoistic concern. I argue the latter explanation is more plausible. And I do not think this pattern of interest is limited to reporters. Imagine yourself in Cahalan's predicament before the disease took hold. But instead of being surprised, imagine you know you'll abruptly lose your psychological faculties for a month. Would this information make it less rational for you to plan for your future during the disease? I suspect many of us would make substantial sacrifices now to ensure we were well cared for during such a disease. And many of us, like Cahalan, would be motivated in a self-interested way to try to reconnect with our ill selves after the ordeal. This is the first problem with Simple Connectedness: in many cases it gets the direction of dependence wrong.

[20] Cahalan (2013).

The second problem with the Simple Connectedness Hypothesis is that there are well-studied cases where it falsely predicts diminished concern. Parfit, McMahan, and other proponents of the psychological connectedness accounts of egoistic concern typically defend the criterion by asking you to imagine a radical change, then judge how interested you would be in your life after the change, and reflect on whether this concern is reasonable. The examples almost always involve a change with a negative moral or social valence. Either you lose your autonomy during the change (i.e., you contract amnesia or you are to be restrained and tortured). Or you change in such a way as to join a class that is typically accorded less social respect (i.e., you become elderly or you become cognitively disabled). Or you change in such a way as to join a class that many readers would find morally repugnant (i.e., you transform from a generous socialist to a greedy oligarch or you transform from a human into a vampire).[21]

But the Simple Connectedness Hypothesis predicts that our egoistic concern will also diminish when the psychological disruptions are neutral or moral/social improvements. Is this right? Consider a case with a disruption analogous to a brief encephalitic episode but without the element of severe disability. Canadian pianist Glenn Gould was famous for his ability to enter "flow" states while performing. Reporter Robert Krulwich reports the experience of Gould playing Bach's Partita No. 2:

> **Flow:** Glenn Gould, supreme interpreter of Bach, is sitting at his living-room piano on a low, low chair, his nose close to the keys. He's at his Canadian country house in his bathrobe. Through the window, you catch snatches of his back yard. It's a windy day and he's got a coffee cup sitting on the piano top. He's working on a Bach partita, not just playing it, but singing along in his swinging baritone. As he plays, he gets so totally, totally lost in the music that suddenly, smack in the middle of a passage, with no warning, for no apparent reason, his left hand flips up, touches his head; he stands up, and walks in what looks like a trance to the window. There's an eerie silence. Then, in the quiet, you hear the Bach leaking out of him. He's still playing it, but in his head, he's scatting the beats. Then he turns, wanders back, sits down, and his fingers pick

[21] Parfit (1984: 327) and Chapter 1 of Paul (2014).

> up right where his voice left off, but now with new energy, like he's found a switch and switched it.[22]

During his "rapture" Gould is psychologically disconnected from his previous selves. He's so absorbed in the music that he is unaware of his surroundings. He cannot call to mind memories. His personality is significantly altered. He is completely disinterested in the future. And his actions lack any conscious intention. "Flow" states like this are the subject of significant research in positive psychology.[23] Skilled surgeons report entering such states during long procedures; in one case a surgeon was so absorbed as to be unaware that the operating room ceiling had collapsed. Athletes report entering such a state during intense competition.

Presumably entering "flow" does not diminish egoistic concern. For instance, a surgeon wouldn't take less credit for a complicated procedure performed while in this disconnected state. Knowing that you will flow during your marathon does not make the experience less important to you now. But the Simple Connectedness Hypothesis predicts that flow would diminish egoistic concern.

You might think that the duration of the gap makes a difference. So consider a case where there is a longer psychological disconnect, analogous to Cahalan's break:

> **Meditative Retreat:** Jonathan has booked a month-long meditation retreat in Sedona, Arizona. In his civilian life, Jonathan is an extroverted and stressed-out lawyer. But during the retreat, he will enter a month-long state of flow. He'll be acutely aware of his breathing and bodily movements. He will think of neither the future nor the past. He won't have goals or intentions. His mind will be "quiet." He knows he will become relaxed and pacific, at least for the duration of the retreat.

Should Jonathan now be less concerned for himself during the retreat? Most of us, I suspect, think not. Indeed, after the retreat, when Jonathan gets back to his stressed, extroverted default, it would be normal for him to identify just as strongly with his calm, pensive retreat self.

You might also think the encephalitic and flow cases differ because in the latter cases the changes are intended but in the former case they

[22] Quoted directly from Krulwich (2014).
[23] Nakamura and Csikszentmihalyi (2002).

are not. Intention is one form of psychological connection. McMahan leans on intention connections to explain why self-improvement would be rational on his version of the psychological connectedness theory.[24] But we can also imagine the flow cases in a way where Gould or Jonathan just "slip" into these states of absorption and tranquility. Unintentional flow does not seem significantly more disruptive to egoistic concern than intentional flow.

A more salient difference between the encephalitis case and the flow cases concerns the culturally mediated moral worth we assign to the agents in the episodes of radical change. In the encephalitis case, Cahalan is an object of pity. She's seriously disabled, dependent upon her caregivers, and emotionally hostile. In the flow cases, Gould is demonstrating virtuosity. Jonathan is becoming his calmer, more introspective, and "better" self. Episodes of psychological disconnect that are morally neutral or moral improvements do not seem to diminish egoistic concern. This suggests another hypothesis for the basis of egoistic concern, which we might call:

> **The Moral Valence Hypothesis:** We will have diminished egoistic concern for any selves who are psychologically dissimilar or causally disconnected from our present self only if those selves have perceived diminished moral capacity or diminished social/moral worth, where such worth might be mediated by cultural assumptions.

There is direct empirical evidence of the Moral Valence Hypothesis in the so-called "Phineas Gage" effect in psychology. Phineas Gage was a railway worker who in 1848 survived an accident where an iron spike was driven through his frontal lobe, permanently and radically altering his personality. His case became a focal point for work on the biological underpinnings of personality and emotion. Subjects in a series of Gage-inspired personality psychology studies are asked to imagine one of two scenarios. In the first, a protagonist (named Phineas) suffers a brain injury and corresponding psychological disruption. As a result Phineas becomes significantly crueler. In these cases, subjects are less likely to report that Phineas is the same individual after the ordeal. But if instead asked to imagine Phineas becoming significantly *kinder* after his brain injury, subjects are more likely to report that he is the same

[24] See Section 1.5.2 of McMahan (2002).

individual.[25] Third-party judgments of personal persistence are sensitive to the moral valence of the psychological changes.

Other studies suggest that we have a robust moral valence when it comes to attributing responsibility and agency, sometimes called the "Pollyanna Principle" after the relentlessly optimistic character in Eleanor Porter's novel *Pollyanna*. George Newman, Paul Bloom, and Joshua Knobe conducted a series of experiments measuring our attitudes about whether some behaviors are manifestations of an agent's "true self" rather than a reflection of some external feature of the agent's situation. Subjects are more likely to attribute motivation to an agent's "true self" when the behavior is perceived as morally valuable. And they are more likely to assign a diminished role to an agent's "true self" when the behavior is perceived as immoral.[26] This study, among others, lends support to the view that we have a positivity bias in our judgments about personal persistence—namely, we tend to think true selves are fundamentally moral. This positivity bias offers further evidence for the Moral Valence Hypothesis. We are less able to see our "true selves" present in an imagined scenario where psychological volatility has perceived negative moral consequences.[27]

Note that these effects hold whether the qualitative personality changes are intentional or accidental, temporary (as in the flow cases) or permanent (as in the Gage cases).

4.6 Egoistic Concern and Bias

With these effects in mind, let's return to the revised Concern Argument:

(1*) There is some criterion C (like psychological connectedness) that determines your rational egoistic concern, and it comes in degrees.

[25] Tobia (2015). [26] See Newman et al. (2014).

[27] Korsgaard hints at a responsibility-focused hypothesis like this in her criticism of Parfit, Williams, and the usual cases invoked in the debates about egoistic concern: "These writers usually emphasize the facts that after the surgical intervention we are altered, we have changed. But surely part of what creates the sense of lost identity is that the person is changed by *intervention*, from outside. The stories might affect us differently if we imagined changes initiated by the person herself, as a result of her own choice. Authorial psychological connectedness is consistent with drastic changes, provided those changes are the result of actions by the person herself or reactions for which she is responsible." Section IV of Korsgaard (1989).

(2*) It is prudentially rational to discount events based on the degree to which those events have C.
(3) Given that you are a normally developing agent, as events are scheduled in the far future, C will tend to hold to a lesser and lesser degree. (The Qualitative Volatility Assumption)
C. As events are scheduled in the far future, it is prudentially rational to discount them.

In the previous section, I offered support for the Moral Valence Hypothesis. Briefly: diminished psychological connections predict diminished egoistic concern *only* when the change is also accompanied by a loss of moral or social standing. And unqualified psychological connectedness does not accurately predict our patterns of egoistic concern. This is evidence against premise (1*) of the Concern Argument, at least insofar as simple psychological connectedness is put forward as the candidate for C. There are many cases where you are unlikely to judge diminished psychological connection as a reasonable basis for discounting.

It is also evidence against (2*). Our positivity bias is a *bias*. It is a valuing attitude that is sensitive to features of the situation that are not reason-giving. Premise (2*) of the Concern Argument is only plausible if you think the qualitative basis for your egoistic concern is reasonable. But once we realize our judgments about egoistic concern exhibit this moral valence, we shouldn't think these judgments give us good reasons to discount. It simply isn't the case that we are only authors of the morally valuable chapters of our lives.[28] I argued in the previous chapter that rationality requires a certain threshold of non-arbitrariness in our reasons. So it requires that we adopt a unified attitude towards the cases. Either you should care just as much about your encephalitic self or such intensive yoga retreats are never in your self-interest. I submit that in response to the tension, we are more likely to seek a less demanding (and less volatile) basis for egoistic concern.

Are these problems specific to the psychological connectedness theory? We can likewise imagine someone planning around a radical change in her body (if bodily connectedness is the basis of concern) or planning

[28] Unless you have a radically voluntarist conception of personal persistence, such that you think it is possible to metaphysically omit yourself from events with a negative moral or social valence.

around radical restructuring of her brain (if neuro-connectedness is the basis of concern). There is less empirical work on how our attitudes about bodily or neural volatility affect our egoistic concern, but there is some reason to expect they exhibit the same phenomenon of moral valence. Egoistic concern is likely to diminish if you imagine your body will be radically altered by amputation. But egoistic concern will remain stable if you imagine your body altered by radical weight loss. Egoistic concern is likely to diminish if you imagine suffering brain damage that makes you somewhat crueler. But it is likely to remain stable if you imagine that your intensive yoga retreats will result in neural rewiring. These hypotheses are testable, just as the hypotheses about the psychological basis of egoistic concern are. They demonstrate, at the very least, that there is insufficient evidence that a qualitative criterion for concern can be found that satisfies both (1*) and (2*) of the Concern Argument.

This leads us back to the more general methodological worry with the Concern Argument. Philosophers have a nasty habit of telling people what they care about. Using thought experiments that might double as science-fiction plots, Parfit, McMahan, Velleman, and others try to motivate one or another theory of the basis of rational egoistic concern, at the same time using these intuitions to offer evidence about what matters to us vis-à-vis being a self over time. If you enter a teletransporter that copies your mind into a new body, would you care if the old body were destroyed? No? You have a psychological connectedness view of selfhood. If your brain were dissected at the corpus callosum and each hemisphere were transplanted in a new body, which of the bodies would be entitled to your assets? Would you be willing to give each new brain hemisphere half of your estate? Then you have a neuro-connectedness view. One thing we know about our intuitions in such thought experiments is that they are highly sensitive to how the cases are described.[29] Told one way, it might strike you as though you were traveling through space-time, splitting in two, or switching bodies. Told another way, you stay right where you are but undergo a radical change. The shiftiness of these thought experiments means they have never been great evidence for a theory of egoistic concern.

[29] See for instance Williams (1970) on the "changing bodies" thought experiments.

What *is* good evidence for a theory of rational egoistic concern? The empirical studies cited above are a great start, at least insofar as we think our ordinary patterns of egoistic concern are rationally defensible. The studies indicate a bias in our attributions of persistence and patterns of concern. Indeed, to the extent that debates about the metaphysics of personal identity have turned on data about rational egoistic concern, it is astounding how infrequently philosophers rely on empirical data about the conditions under which subjects think they have reason to care about qualitative volatility.

We'd also do well, I think, to take seriously the received wisdom from Chapter 1 about the rationality of distant future planning. For thousands of years and across cultures, it has been taken as a norm that agents ought to plan for their futures, even when those futures are quite a long ways off.[30] Whatever candidate properties we advance as being the rational basis of egoistic concern, they must be reconciled with the robust assumption that we ought to pay significant attention to our self-interest over the long run. The Concern Argument for personal discounting faces a stiff challenge from the outset.

So what should we care about when we care self-interestedly? An obvious candidate for a qualitative basis of egoistic concern is the mere persistence and connectedness of our consciousness (and, indirectly, whatever is needed to realize our consciousness). This would justify Cahalan's reaction in the encephalitis case—she may not have her personality through the ordeal but she knows she was still awake and having experiences. Flow cases, likewise, do not disrupt mere consciousness. The trouble is, as we posit a weaker and more tolerant basis for rational egoistic concern, premise (3) of the Concern Argument looks less and less plausible. While our psychologies might be volatile over long periods of time, our consciousness persists relatively unperturbed.

4.7 The Persistence Argument

So far we've considered two forms of volatility that might make a rational difference to distant future planning. The first is outcome volatility—the

[30] Or in the case of some Far Eastern cultures, agents ought to plan for the futures of their particular families.

range of probabilities assigned to potential outcomes of a choice. It is rational to discount events probabilistically, and as a matter of course, we often should deem events less and less probable as they are scheduled further in the future. But this is not enough to explain why we save so little, since most of us are quite optimistic about our survival in the next few decades. The second is qualitative personal volatility—changes in whatever properties are a reasonable basis for egoistic concern. In the previous three sections, I raised doubts that we are qualitatively volatile in any way that would make a difference to rational egoistic concern. We turn now to a third, somewhat more nebulous form of volatility that might justify personal discounting: numerical volatility.

To introduce this form of volatility, consider another true story:

Brain on Ice: In 2011, Kim Suozzi, age twenty-three, was diagnosed with terminal brain cancer. Suozzi had some training in neuroscience and had been involved in research on connectomes—the neural networks that some scientists believe house an individual's consciousness. Suozzi contracted with a company called Alcor to cryogenically preserve her brain upon death. In January 2013, she slipped into a coma and was pronounced dead. Technicians from Alcor separated Suozzi's head from her torso, pumped her brain with cryoprotectant, and stored it in a container in their facility. The plan required creating a trust of $80,000 to keep her brain preserved. Suozzi's hope was that at some future time, technology will advance enough that her connectome can be mapped and simulated. She hoped such a procedure might bring her back.[31]

Suppose in fifty years we will have the technology to map the connectome of a preserved brain. And suppose Suozzi's connectome will be simulated in new brain tissue. Will Suozzi come back? Was Suozzi rational to create a trust for such an event before she succumbed to her cancer? You might think it is an all-or-nothing matter whether Suozzi (or anyone) could be revived in this way. If you think existence is an all-or-nothing affair, then there is a determinate fact about whether a revived cryogenic brain is or isn't identical to its pre-mortem donor. In this case, the riskiness of

[31] Amy Harmon, "A Dying Woman's Hope in Cryonics and a Future," *The New York Times Magazine*, Sept. 12, 2015.

freezing a brain is represented as a form of outcome volatility—it is hard to be confident that the procedure will work.

But you may also think that existence over time is not an all-or-nothing affair. The properties that determine whether you remain you over a series of changes can come in degrees. As a result, it can be a matter of degree how you (or anyone) would persist through an adventure like Suozzi's. Suppose that a person's persistence over time is determined by her connectome—she survives over time just in case there is a series of connections between her neural network at one time and a neural network at another. Connectome relations can presumably hold in degrees. Between 2010 and 2011—before her disease—Suozzi's connectome changed little. But as her cancer progressed, her brain changed rapidly. The cryogenic freezing process further damaged her connectome. Any neural network built from her brain after 2013 will be related to her 2011 connectome, but tenuously. You might think that means that if Suozzi is revived, the resulting person will be much less Suozzi.

A gradualist view of persistence like this suggests another potential defense of personal discounting:

The Persistence Argument for Personal Discounting

(1) There is some criterion C that determines your persistence over time, and it comes in degrees.

(2) It is prudentially rational to discount a future event based on the degree to which you will be affected by that event.

(3) For any plausible candidate for your C, as events are scheduled further in the future, C will tend to hold to a lesser degree. (The Numerical Volatility Assumption)

C. As events are scheduled further in the future, it is prudentially rational to discount them.

As with the Concern Argument, candidates for C include psychological connectedness, bodily connectedness, or embodied consciousness. But unlike that argument, the Persistence Argument says nothing about what qualities you care about into the future. Instead, it turns on how you rationally care about the "amount" of yourself into the future.

This is a potential route to defending personal discounting. But all three premises of the Persistence Argument are deeply controversial.

How should we understand Premise (1)? You might think that facts about your persistence are susceptible of indeterminacy. When your persistence comes in degrees, this means there is an increase in indeterminacy about your persistence every time C is disrupted. Call this the *indeterminacy* reading of criterion C. This reading rules out the possibility that your identity is determined by something that cannot come in degrees, like having the same soul over time. Many philosophers—myself included—have the view that existence over time is an all-or-nothing matter. For anything, after any change, there is a determinate fact about whether the thing undergoing the change has survived.[32] And it is never indeterminate how many things exist, selves included.[33]

On the indeterminacy reading, premises (1) and (3) also require a dramatic departure from our ordinary self-conceptions. For instance, few of us believe that our age is radically indeterminate, but if (1) and (3) are true, the parallel reasoning applies equally to our past. As events are scheduled further in the past, it happened less to me. So I should not be so quick to assert that I am thirty-four years old. At best I was indeterminately present in the 1980s. If we assume psychological connectedness is the relevant C, then when Susannah Cahalan relates stories about her adult life, she should take care to note gaps like the encephalitic episode when she is at best indeterminately the protagonist. I've maintained that theories of prudential rationality should be prima facie conservative with respect to what they entail about our self-conceptions. That is, any normative argument with a controversial metaphysical premise is likely to be question-begging (or at least deeply unpersuasive) because it is typically much easier to revise our confidence about what it is rational to do or prefer than it is to revise our confidence about what we are.

The Persistence Argument is also at risk of equivocation. Premise (2) looks plausible when we interpret "degrees" in terms of probabilistic volatility. We might be uncertain as to what our persistence conditions are, and so we might not know if we could survive the death of our organic brain. Any of us with a healthy open-mindedness about the potential for an afterlife are likely worried about whether our persistence conditions are flexible enough to allow us to come back. But we need a different interpretation of the relevant volatility to make the Persistence Argument

[32] Sullivan (2012a). [33] Sider (2001: 120–39).

logically valid—we have to interpret it as a prediction about how much you are the person in the future event, where this "amount of you" can be increased or decreased at a given time. Call this the *quantitative reading* of criterion C. On this view, facts about existence and persistence are always determinate, but selves are like fast-food beverages: they come in different sizes. So Suozzi could determinately survive by having her connectome simulated, but there will be less of her after the procedure.

Maybe this is a metaphysical option. But it is far less clear that such quantitative considerations are any part of prudential rationality. Indeed, there is an argument that amounts of self at a time should not matter for rational egoistic concern, as long as there is some self to be concerned with. Suppose for reductio you endorsed the following principle:

> **Synchronic Aggregation:** A rational agent will apportion egoistic concern to a self (or selves) at a time based on amount of self (or selves) who exist at that time.

The principle seems plausible enough if the only values for "amounts of self" at issue are determinate and binary: 0 or 1. But matters get trickier if we start to assume that selves can come in other denominations. For instance, how do we assign a self-interested value to an outcome at a time if selves come in increasing denominations?

> **Saving with Fission:** Suppose I am presented with two investment opportunities. On Opportunity 1: I will pay $300 into an account now, and I will be allowed to withdraw $1,000 three years later. On Opportunity 2: I will pay $300 into an account now, enter a personal fission machine once, split into two selves, and each of my daughter selves will receive $550 dollars three years later.

Synchronic Aggregation seems to give me a reason to prefer Opportunity 2. On this option I have twice as many selves and, if I aggregate their interests, it seems the investment is as good (from a self-interested standpoint) as the promise of being compensated $1,100 later for a $300 investment now. This assumes that rational egoistic concern recommends making short-term sacrifices when they will be compensated in the long run (once probabilities have been taken into account).[34] Perhaps facts about

[34] Again, see Brink (2010: 360–6).

diminishing marginal utility for money would even further recommend Opportunity 2. Each of your daughter selves is likely to get more pleasure per dollar on this distribution scheme.

But this reasoning cannot be correct. And the problems get even more stark when the "amounts of self" are allowed to grow further. Suppose I am given Opportunity 3: I will pay $300 into an account now, enter the fission machine seven times, and split into 128 daughter selves, each of whom will receive $8.60 three years later. Prudential rationality does not compel me to prefer this option. Indeed, the possibility of fission seems most closely analogous to the possibility of a firm splitting its stock. There can be more denominations, but splitting results in no increase in value.

So either prudential rationality does not recommend making sacrifices now for later, self-involved compensation. Or rational agents will prefer the fissioning options in the cases above. Or only diminishing quantity is ever significant. Or—most plausibly—Synchronic Aggregation is false. It might be false because we always have at most one determinate self (the option I favor). Or it might be that no matter how much self we have in reality, we must treat it as one for the sake of assigning value in rational tradeoffs. On either of these last approaches, the Persistence Argument for personal discounting is unconvincing. Neither numerical nor qualitative volatility supply robust reasons for future discounting. Premise (2) of the Arbitrariness Argument stands.

4.8 The Two-Part Case for Future Neutrality

Near bias has been a topic of perennial interest to philosophers, psychologists, and economists, and there is a burgeoning interdisciplinary consensus on how to measure it and what mechanisms likely give rise to it. With the exception of figures like Bentham, Parfit, and McMahan, there is also significant agreement that near bias is not rationally permissible. As I have argued in the past three chapters, this normative claim can be defended with at least two arguments. First we worked through the Life-Saving Argument. In brief: to the extent that prudential rationality is a matter of planning to have your life go well, it is irrational to discount the distant future. Then we worked through the Arbitrariness Argument. In brief: to the extent that a prudentially rational agent's preferences aren't sensitive to arbitrary differences, it is irrational to discount the distant future.

Having laid out the case for future neutrality, we now turn to a far more neglected time bias: bias towards the future. In the next part of this book, I will argue that a parallel two-pronged case can be mounted for *past neutrality*. A prudentially rational agent shouldn't be sensitive to whether events are already over and done with.

5

Preferences about the Past

"Things past redress are now with me past care."

Shakespeare, *Richard II*, Act II, Scene 3

5.1 A Negotiating Tip for Accident Victims

Suppose you were riding your bike last week and a negligent driver ran a stop sign, hitting you. You are now in hospital with a treatable and very painful compound fracture. You'll need surgery, but you should make a complete recovery. You plan to sue the driver for your medical bills and for compensation for your pain and suffering. Assume there is no impending deadline to file your complaint. Should you wait until you've healed to seek damages?

Evidence from social psychology indicates that you should make haste to press your case while your pain is still present, at least insofar as you care about money. You'll tend to ask for significantly more compensation for a present pain than you will for one that is already passed. Conversely, your assailant would do well to encourage you to wait and heal before you name your price.

In an intriguing 2008 study in *Psychological Science*, Eugene Caruso, Daniel Gilbert, and Timothy Wilson used judgments about fitting compensation to observe differences in our attitudes towards past and future pains.[1] For instance, they found subjects more heavily discount the compensation value of onerous tasks they've already performed compared with tasks they are scheduled to perform:

My Boring Data Entry: One hundred twenty-one participants on the Harvard University campus were asked to imagine that they had agreed

[1] Caruso et al. (2008).

to spend five hours entering data into a computer and to indicate how much money it would be fair for them to receive. Some participants imagined that they had completed the work one month previously, and others imagined that they would complete the work one month in the future. Participants believed that they should receive 101% more money for work they would do one month later ($125.04) than for identical work that they had done one month previously ($62.20).[2]

The compensation studies are a clever way to measure a phenomenon that should be very familiar—we tend to prefer bad events in our lives to be over and done with and we tend to prefer good events to be present or future. Still, these studies are, at best, an indirect way of measuring our attitudes to the past. And if you think there is something rationally suspect about asking for less compensation as a painful experience shifts to the past—well, read on, because I agree.

5.2 Bias Towards the Future

Curiously, while we have seen philosophers from vastly different traditions who have been keen to offer arguments criticizing or defending near bias, there are scant parallel arguments criticizing or defending our preferences about the past.[3] Maybe this is because it is even more an article of received wisdom that you shouldn't care about events that have already occurred. We see such advice repeatedly in literature. In the Bible: "Forgetting what is behind and straining toward what is ahead, I press toward the goal to win the prize for which God has called me . . ." (Philippians 3:13–14). In Shakespeare: "Things without all remedy should be without regard: *what's done is done*" (Lady Macbeth in *Macbeth*). In modern English: "Don't cry over spilled milk." The received wisdom is do not bother yourself with things you cannot change, most notably the past.

I suspect that preferences about the past have also been neglected by philosophers and psychologists because of conceptual confusions about

[2] Caruso et al. (2008).

[3] Some philosophers explicitly assume that we should care less about past events. Hence Christopher Heathwood: a future-biased person is "completely reasonable in preferring that his pain be in the past. In fact, even his no longer caring at all that it occurred is perfectly fitting—not at all inappropriate. Why should he care about it now? It is over and done with" (Heathwood 2008: 56–7). See also Schlesinger (1975).

what a past-directed preference is, how it is to be detected, and what rational considerations could possibly be brought to bear on such preferences. Preferences about the past will be the subject of the next three chapters. In this chapter, I will consider whether we can sensibly ascribe agents a discount function for past experiences. I'll argue that when it comes to pains and pleasures, our past discounting is likely absolute—we do not value them at all. I will also consider and dismiss some worries that the very concept of a past-directed preference is incoherent.

After laying the conceptual foundations, in subsequent chapters I will offer two arguments that this time bias is irrational. Each argument parallels one of the main arguments against near bias that we have surveyed. In the process, I will develop the philosophical case for past neutrality: rational agents do not discount events merely because they have already occurred (or would have occurred). This may seem deeply counterintuitive, but in Chapter 8 I'll offer a unified theory of why both past discounting and distant future discounting seem so tempting, even if they are ultimately attitudes we should seek to overcome.

5.3 Determining Discount Functions for the Past

In Chapter 1, we saw that a future discounter's value function takes three inputs—the amount of time between a future event and the present, the amount an agent would value some experience if it were present, and a future discount function—and determines a present, discounted value for a future event. And we defined a future-neutral agent as an agent that has no future discount function; you are future-neutral if you value some future event just as though it were happening now. A past-directed value function likewise takes three variables—the amount of time that has elapsed between a past event and the present, the amount you would value the event if it were present, and some past discount function—and it determines the present, discounted value for some past event. As before, if the present value would be positive, the discount function decreases. If it is negative, the discount function increases its value. Suppose you have an exponential past discount function for vacations. And suppose right now you'd prefer a vacation in India to a vacation to Milwaukee (assuming both were happening presently). If the trip to India ended yesterday, you

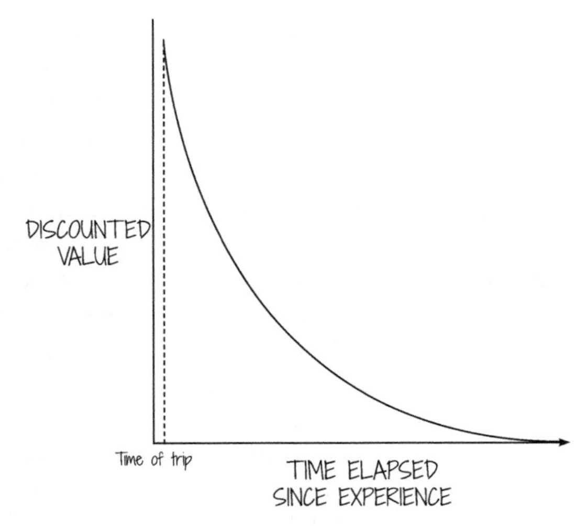

Figure 5.1 Past discounting for vacations

might still prefer it to a present vacation to Milwaukee. But if the India trip happened a decade ago, you'd prefer just about any good present vacation to it. On this model (represented in Figure 5.1), as vacations recede into the past you value them less.

We will say you are *future-biased* if you have some discount function for past experiences. The discount function might be gradually decreasing, similar to the exponential and hyperbolic functions that psychologists use to model near bias. Or it might be some fixed rate, like all past experiences counting for half. You are *past-neutral* if you have no such past discount function—you value any past experience just as much as if it were presently occurring.

As with future discounting, we might hypothesize that we employ different discount functions for different kinds of past events. Other than the Caruso, Gilbert, and Wilson study, there has been little work in psychology trying to identify these rates. In fact, this is an area where social scientific methods can be of considerable help to philosophy (and vice versa). In the absence of such empirical studies, we can still offer thought experiments to gesture at what those discount functions might be. And here we discover some ways that future bias manifests differently from near bias.

In the case of "pure" experiences of pains and pleasures, it seems that our discount functions are absolute: for any amount of time that has elapsed, we assign no value to a merely past painful experience or pleasurable experience.[4] To see why our discount functions for pains and pleasures are absolute, first consider a thought experiment from Derek Parfit:

> **My Past and Future Operations:** I am in some hospital, to have some kind of surgery. Since this is completely safe, and always successful, I have no fears about the effects. The surgery may be brief, or it may instead take a long time. Because I have to co-operate with the surgeon, I cannot have anesthetics. I have had this surgery once before, and I can remember how painful it is. Under the new policy, because the operation is so painful, patients are now afterwards made to forget it . . .
>
> I have just woken up. I cannot remember going to sleep. I ask my nurse if it has been decided when my operation is to be, and how long it must take. She says that she knows the facts about both me and another patient, but that she cannot remember which facts apply to whom. She can tell me only that the following is true. I may be the patient who had his operation yesterday. In that case, my operation was the longest ever performed, lasting ten hours. I may instead be the patient who is to have a short operation later today. It is either true that I did suffer for ten hours, or true that I shall suffer for one hour.
>
> I ask the nurse to find out which is true. While she is away, it is clear to me which I prefer to be true. If I learn that the first is true, I shall be greatly relieved. (Parfit 1984: 165)

Parfit assumes in this scenario an agent would prefer a more painful surgery in the past rather than a less painful surgery in the future.

But if you have a non-absolute past discount function for pain, then your preferences will be sensitive to how much time has elapsed between the past surgery and the present.[5] For instance, if you are an exponential past discounter, your preferences can be modeled with a function like Figure 5.2. Here the Y-axis measures the discounted disvalue of the events. Your preferences will change at the time in between the surgeries if the curves cross. So in this example, whether you prefer the past surgery depends on how much time has elapsed, since at some point between the

[4] We may, however, value present or future memories of these experiences which themselves convey pain or pleasure.

[5] This argument was originally given in Greene and Sullivan (2015).

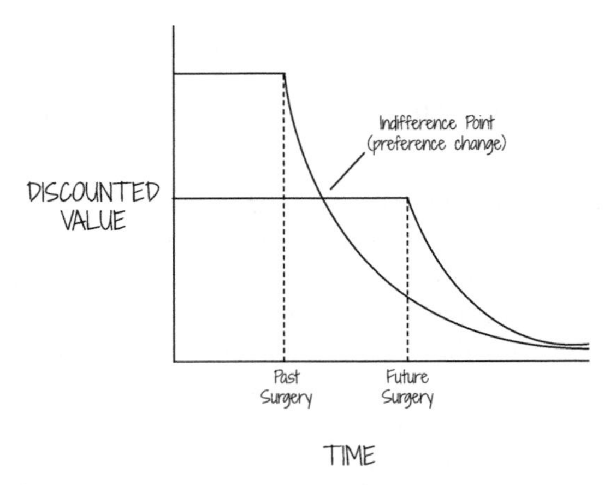

Figure 5.2 Past discounting for Parfit's Operations

two surgeries the curves representing disvalue cross. To keep it simple, imagine that the point at which they cross is about five hours after the more painful surgery. And imagine the future surgery is half as bad as the past one. In this case, if it has been four hours since the more painful surgery, the model predicts that you would prefer the less painful future surgery. However, if it has been six hours, you will prefer the more painful past surgery.

But in Parfit's original example, it is supposed to be absurd for anyone to hope for a future surgery. It is even more absurd for your hopes to rest on how much time has elapsed since when the past surgery would have taken place.[6] Similar cases can be devised for experiences of pleasure. For these reasons it seems implausible to model past discounting for pains or pleasures using any non-absolute discount function.[7] Of course, present memories of the events might still matter a great deal. But the event of

[6] Stranger still, if an agent both is near-biased and employs a past discount function, we can find situations where the agent would prefer a *more* painful future surgery to a less painful past surgery, assuming the future surgery were scheduled far enough in the future and the past surgery in the recent enough past.

[7] Does it matter if the non-absolute discount function is non-continuous? Suppose as soon as the pain is past, you discount by a permanent rate of 1/100th. In this case, there is no time between the past and potential future surgery when your preferences switch. But such a discount function is still psychologically unrealistic. For instance, it predicts you would prefer a 1-hour surgery tomorrow to a 101-hour surgery fifty years ago that you have no recollection of and suffer no present consequences from.

remembering the surgery and the event of having had it are distinct, and they are assigned different values.

Tom Dougherty thinks it is implausible to assume we discount past pains and pleasures absolutely, since this would mean you "would (also) be indifferent between a childhood full of pleasant days of adventure and friendship and a childhood as a victim of bullying."[8] But it is important to distinguish hedonic and non-hedonic discounting. When you care about having had a happy childhood, do you care about whether there were pains or pleasures in that time or do you care about whether there are other goods in your past—for instance, opportunities to grow, to have childhood accomplishments and relationships, and an early life story that does not include episodes of victimization? When it comes to goods besides pains and pleasures, it is harder to establish if we have any past discount function. For instance, Thomas Hurka argues that when it comes to eudaemonistic goods it is psychologically unrealistic to posit a discount function. He offers us a parallel of Parfit's amnesia thought experiment, this time involving scientific achievements:

> **My Past and Future Discoveries:** Imagine that, awakening in hospital with temporary amnesia, you are told that you are either a scientist who made a major discovery last year or a different scientist who will make a minor discovery next year. You will surely hope you are the first scientist. You will want your life to contain the greatest scientific achievement possible, regardless of its temporal location.[9]

I take it as an empirical question whether Hurka is right about our lack of discounting for achievements or whether Dougherty's right about how we value our childhood. We could (and should) gather empirical evidence for my claim that we discount pains and pleasures absolutely. Such studies are difficult because it is difficult to tease apart how we value experiences themselves from how we value presently occurring memories of those past experiences. Our past typically affects our present well-being through memories, which is why Parfit needs amnesia in his thought experiment.

We should also be cautious about interpreting indirect thought experiments like the Caruso, Gilbert, and Wilson compensation studies as

[8] Dougherty (2015, fn6). [9] Hurka (1996, 61).

measuring the kinds of past discount functions defined here. It is better to read these studies as establishing our "exchange rates" for comparing pains and pleasures to goods with temporally stable values (like money).[10] In the next chapter, we will look at how such time-biased exchange rates lead to problems for rational planning. These caveats aside, Parfit's Operations thought experiment gives us some evidence that when we directly discount past pains and pleasures, we do it absolutely.

5.4 Do Subjective Probabilities Matter?

In defining what it is to be near-biased, I took pains to distinguish this form of discounting from probabilistic discounting—discounting the value of a future event based on the subjective probability you assign to it occurring. We can assign subjective probabilities to past events as well. For instance, the amnesiac who wakes up in Parfit's case should figure that there is a 50% chance he suffered a horrible surgical ordeal yesterday. Do you discount past events based on the likelihood that they occurred? In the case of pains and pleasures, if the previous argument for absolute discounting is sound, then probably not. If merely being past makes a painful or pleasurable event valueless, then there is no way to discount it even further based on the likelihood that it happened.

In the case of other kinds of goods, the answer is not so straightforward. Suppose Hurka is right and we are temporally neutral when it comes to achievements. You think there is a 25% chance you made a major discovery. Would you trade this state of affairs for one where you are certain to have made a discovery that is half as good? If so, then there is evidence that you discount past states of affairs based on risk. But the example is confounded by the fact that you cannot "trade" your actual past for a counterfactual past like this. And risk discounting only makes sense when our preferences are connected to choices. Which raises an even more central difficulty for how to understand past discounting—does it even make sense to have a preference over something you cannot control? And how could such a preference ever be irrational?

[10] Thanks to Johann Frick for discussing this point with me.

5.5 Preferences and Control

You might think that rationality only constrains preferences which are action-guiding. If you can't do anything about your preference, then you can't be criticized for it either. More precisely: a preference is only rational or irrational *relative* to a potential choice. When no choice is involved, the attitudes are rationally neutral or are better understood as desires or wishes. Any desire or wish is permissible insofar as it has no practical effects on an agent's choices. Since the past is settled, it doesn't make sense to ascribe agents irrational preferences about the past. We can call this the *control constraint* on preferences.[11]

The control constraint can be both too restrictive and too permissive (in different contexts). Why can it be overly restrictive? Well, why think that an agent can only form a rational preference with respect to a particular choice? As illustrated with cases in the Introduction, I think it makes more sense to think of preferences as reflected not only in the choices we make, but in the value to us of learning that certain states of affairs do or do not obtain. While Sam may have no say whatsoever over whether there will be torrential rain in New York tomorrow, he can prefer the state of affairs where it rains to the one where it does not rain. And he'd be irrational in preferring that it rain if he also prefers that his picnic in Central Park not be ruined. Our everyday notion of a preference does not require agents to have control over relata. And it would be too restrictive to build it into our definition of preferences that we could never criticize Sam for preferring the weather not break his way. In adopting this broader concept of a preference we can partly take inspiration from Richard Jeffrey, who understands preferences on the "news value" model: to say that A is ranked higher than B means that the agent would welcome the news that A is true more than he would welcome the news that B is true.[12]

Evaluating preferences only with respect to particular choices can also lead to problems with understanding the Success principle for rationality, and in this sense the control constraint is also too permissive. I'll give some more developed examples of this in the next chapter, but here is

[11] This material is excerpted from Section 5 of Finochiarro and Sullivan (2016).

[12] Jeffrey (1983, 82). Jeffrey does not, however, permit meaningful preferences over metaphysical impossibilities. More on this in Chapter 7. I am thankful to Tom Dougherty for raising this option in discussion.

one to get us started. In decision theory, an agent is "money pumped" if she makes a series of trades which guarantees that she is worse off than if she hadn't made the trades. In a diachronic money pump case, an agent faces a series of choices, has a clear preference in each individual choice based on her interests at the time of choice, but jointly her pattern of choices leads to a certain loss. Further, the certainty of loss can be observed before the series of trades occurs. We saw in Chapter 1 that hyperbolically near-biased vacationers have such preferences. Dougherty offers an argument that agents with certain forms of risk-aversion and a tendency to discount the past will also be susceptible to a diachronic money pump—they will accept a series of choices which will result in a sure, avoidable loss.[13] Remember Parfit's Operations case? Here is Dougherty's interesting variant. (It is a bit involved, but the details matter for the logic of the argument.)

> **Pain Insurance:** On Monday, you are admitted into a hospital. You are told you will have one of two courses of operations, but you are not told which. If you have the early course, then you will have a painful, four-hour operation on Tuesday and a painful, one-hour operation on Thursday. If you have the late course, then you will have a painful, three-hour operation on Thursday. After any operation, you will have amnesia for several days, and so you will not be able to remember if you have just had an operation. There is a calendar next to your bed, and so you always know what day it is.
>
> You also have the option of choosing to take pills that work to alleviate pain for the different kinds of treatments. Here are the options:
>
> Pill 1 (Help for the Early Course (4+1)): If you will have the early course, then this pill decreases the length of the pain you experience on Thursday by twenty-nine minutes. If you will have the late course, then the pill increases the length of the pain you experience on Thursday by thirty-one minutes.
>
> Pill 2 (Help for the Late Course (0+3)): If you are having the early course, then this pill increases the length of the pain you experience on Thursday by thirty minutes. If you are having the late course, then the pill decreases the length of the pain you experience on Thursday by thirty minutes.

[13] Dougherty (2011). For criticism and discussion of the case see Section 3 of Greene and Sullivan (2015).

If all you care about is reducing the risk of pain, and the only pain you ever care about is future pain, then you'll take Pill 1 on Monday and Pill 2 on Wednesday. As a result, you are guaranteed to have a minute's extra pain on Thursday and gain absolutely nothing in return. The agonizing arithmetic is shown in the table below.[14]

	Effect of Pill 1	Effect of Pill 2	Effect of Both
You have early (4+1) course	−29 min	30 min	1 min
You have late (0+3) course	31 min	−30 min	1 min

You have been "pain pumped."

We typically do not want to say that someone who makes such deals for certain pain increase is rational. Such an agent's preferences certainly aren't contributing to her long-run success. But if we only evaluate rational preferences relative to particular choices, then we'll be forced to conclude that it is rationally permissible to accept such a series of choices. After all, you have good reasons from risk aversion to want to reduce future pain every time you are offered a pill, and the only pain you can control is future pain.[15] One lesson from the case is that we should be able to criticize whole packages of preferences, even when they are disconnected from particular choices. Moreover, while attitudes about the past may never be action-guiding considered individually, they can be action-guiding in conjunction with your other beliefs and preferences. And to the extent that we think we can measure well-being across time (as the Success principle supposes) rather than only at a time, we must take past discounting attitudes as subject to rational criticism. We will see many examples of this in the next chapter.

We should reject the control constraint and instead take a broader view of preferences that permits past-directed preferences. If you remain unconvinced that what is past redress should not be past care, I'll offer two sets of arguments in the next two chapters. These arguments won't lean heavily on your intuitions about improbable surgeries with amnesia

[14] Dougherty (2011, 528).

[15] But see Hedden (2015a) for an argument that it is rationally permissible to be susceptible of diachronic money pumps.

and pain insurance. Instead, we'll look at problems that past discounters (especially hedonic past discounters) face in resisting temptation, making and sticking to plans, and explaining why death is bad. These are problems all of us face to varying degrees, and a theory of complete temporal neutrality can help us solve them.

6

The No Regrets Argument

> Laws and principles are not for the times when there is no temptation: they are for such moments as this, when body and soul rise in mutiny against their rigour... If at my convenience I might break them, what would be their worth?
>
> Charlotte Brontë, *Jane Eyre*

There is a tendency to think that discounting past pains and pleasures is rationally permissible because there is no way that an agent could end up being worse off for being future-biased. The aim of this chapter is to convince you that this assumption is false. Committed past discounters will make choices that will cause their lives to go less well. If you found the Life-Saving Argument for future neutrality convincing back in Chapter 2, you should go further and think rationality requires past neutrality too.

I'll develop and defend two arguments that show that past discounters will end up worse off as a result of their time bias. The first argument contends that past discounters will end up worse off when they face mixed tradeoffs—scenarios where they are asked to trade experiences of pain and pleasure for a good with a temporally constant value. The second argument contends that past discounters will end up worse off when they try to take into account their anticipated future preferences. Note that in this chapter we'll focus on hedonic experiences—experiences of pain and pleasure—since these are the experiences we most clearly discount. But if there are other goods we exhibit future bias towards, the arguments could be generalized to those as well.

6.1 No Pain, No Gain?

To introduce the first argument, it will be helpful to consider a thought experiment:

Crossfit: Carrie has recently joined the Crossfit craze. She has set as her goal to have one tough workout per day. Before heading to the gym (or "Box," as committed Crossfitters call it) she looks up the workout of the day. The Box has determined that a tough workout today should cost her 45 minutes' worth of suffering. After working out for 45 minutes, she takes a break to consider whether she has (now) done enough to have earned a tough workout. She reasons as follows: "I have put in 45 minutes of suffering, but it is all past pain, so it is worth absolutely nothing to me. I have only earned a tough workout if I have traded something of value for the workout." Carrie reluctantly heads back for some more suffering.[1]

There is something wrong with Carrie's reasoning. In a sense, she is overpaying for her tough workout. But where is she going wrong?

One option is to think we shouldn't measure the value of something like a workout based on the amount of suffering that goes into it. The Crossfit case is an example of a *mixed tradeoff*. You make a mixed tradeoff whenever you trade a painful or pleasurable experience for another kind of good with a relatively temporally invariant value, like a sum of money or the accomplishment of finishing a workout. We make mixed tradeoffs constantly. We trade money for exciting experiences. We trade our labor and sweat for personal goals. We demand monetary compensation for pain and suffering. Any theory of prudential rationality should explain when and why it is rational to prefer one option over another in such a tradeoff.

Another response is to think there is something wrong with Carrie's willingness to discount her suffering once it is in the past. When it comes to figuring out whether she has "done enough" to have earned a tough workout, she should value her past pain and suffering just as much as if it is present. She should not be time-biased when it comes to pains involved in mixed tradeoffs.

In the last chapter, we considered Caruso, Gilbert, and Wilson's compensation studies. These studies do not directly measure past discount functions. Rather, they indirectly measure the exchange rates we think are appropriate in mixed tradeoffs. And they provide further reason to think there is something deeply incoherent about our tendency to discount past

[1] Inspired by cases presented by Dougherty (2015).

pains and pleasures. When we reason about the cases directly (as in Parfit's surgery case), we are disposed to discount past experiences absolutely. But when asked to set an exchange rate for past experiences, many of us think they can be compensated with other goods. There is some value (however small) we think is needed to make us whole after a bicycle accident. But few of us feel the inclination to "pay" the 45 minutes of Crossfit pain all over again. Prudentially rational agents should base their exchange rates on what they think the actual value of the experience is. Either our past pains and pleasures still have just as much value (as the tradeoffs suppose) or they do not (as the Parfit cases suppose). Which is it?

6.2 The Mixed Tradeoff Argument

We can make this mixed tradeoff problem into an explicit argument for past neutrality. Here is the argument, which I call the *Mixed Tradeoff Argument*. The idea is originally due to Dougherty.[2]

The Mixed Tradeoff Argument

(1) For any good and any particular hedonic experience, if you are indifferent between some amount of the good and the experience when it is in the future, then you are rationally required to be indifferent between the same amount of the good and the experience when it is in the past.

(2) You face mixed tradeoffs, and for some exchange rate you are indifferent between the good and the future experience.

(3) If you are indifferent between A and B, and indifferent between B and C, then you are rationally required to be indifferent between A and C.

(C) So you are rationally required to be indifferent between a particular hedonic experience when the experience is in the future and the same hedonic experience when it is in the past.

The conclusion is a form of past neutrality about hedonic experiences. Consider the premises in reverse order. Premise (3) follows from the Consistency standard for prudential rationality—it is an example of the transitivity requirement on preferences.

[2] Dougherty presents the argument using just premises (1) and (3). That version of the argument is invalid unless we assume—as I explicitly add here—that we face mixed tradeoffs and are indifferent in the future-directed versions (Dougherty 2015: 11–12).

Premise (2) merely states that we sometimes face choices where we must decide how to sacrifice pain or pleasure for some other kind of good with a temporally constant value. And when we face such tradeoffs where the pains or pleasures are in the future, we often set such exchange rates. For Carrie, a good workout in the future is worth exactly 45 minutes of suffering.

Why believe Premise (1)? Recall the Success principle that served as the engine of the Life-Saving Argument back in Chapter 2: a rational agent will prefer now that her life going forward go as well as possible. An agent who discounts past hedonic experiences in mixed tradeoffs is going to be worse off in the future than an agent who is past-neutral. Carrie the Crossfitter suffers much more than she needs to for a tough workout, since she never judges she has paid enough.

A past discounter in mixed tradeoffs can also anticipate that she will "cheat" her future selves by committing them to deals which she knows she will regret. Dougherty offers a case demonstrating this:

> **Hippie Tipping:** Victoria is dining at a "progressive" restaurant where customers are allowed to set the price for their meal based on what they think the pleasure of eating is worth to them. Before dining, Victoria decides that the experience of eating her greens and grains is worth $50 to her and commits to paying that. After eating her meal, the experience is in her past and therefore worth little or nothing to Victoria. (Depending on her discount function.) She certainly does not (now) prefer to pay $50 compensation for the experience and regrets agreeing to the rate.[3]

The only way to avoid committing herself to a deal she knows she will come to regret is to commit to being temporally neutral about the value of the experience.

Note that a version of the Mixed Tradeoff problem also affects *near-biased* agents trading temporally constant goods like accomplishments for temporally discounted goods like suffering. Here is a real-life planning trap I often succumb to. Philosophers are typically invited to contribute articles to volumes one to two years in advance of the due date. An original article optimistically takes three months of non-stop research suffering to

[3] Dougherty (2015).

complete. I am often willing to commit to such projects when the deadline is far ahead, because I think the value of the accomplishment (publishing an article) outweighs the anticipated suffering (which I heavily discount at the time of the request). As the deadline approaches, I often regret making the commitment, since I weigh the anticipated suffering much more as it becomes present. In this case, my trouble is that I form an intention with one mixed exchange rate in mind, but I end up "paying" another rate when I act on my plan.

Premise (1) of the Mixed Tradeoff Argument leads us to think more precisely about how our anticipated regrets might serve as reasons for our present preferences. This leads to the second Success-based argument for past neutrality, which I call the *No Regrets Argument*. But before we get to the argument proper, we should pause to consider why prudential rationality might compel us to pay attention to our anticipated future preferences.

6.3 Resisting Temptation

As we've seen, the case against near bias assumes that self-interest is inextricably linked with self-control. In constantly succumbing to temptation, near-biased agents miss out on opportunities which would convey substantially more well-being but also require a significant investment. Which raises the question—how should a rational agent approach temptation? On one way of looking at it, temptation occurs when your emotions cloud your beliefs and considered preferences. For instance, you may believe that it is best to break off an unhealthy relationship. You may have formed a preference to no longer speak with your problematic ex. Then the person calls you and, overcome in the moment, you answer. The Greeks call this giving in to temptation "akrasia"—the phenomenon of knowing what you should do, but being unable to bring yourself to do it.

Some temptation is akratic in this sense, but much temptation is not. Sometimes we just weigh reasons for preferences differently over time. For example:

> **The Second Drink:** I am at a restaurant with a friend. I have already had one Manhattan. If I have another, I will not be able to drive myself home. I will need to pay extra to leave my car in the parking garage overnight. I will be significantly encumbered in tomorrow's

> commute. The waiter comes and offers another round. My friend is keen to indulge. I have some reasons for preferring the second drink to abstaining—it will be refreshing, and I can enjoy more conversation with my friend. I may even think right now that it wouldn't be so bad to leave my car. But if I think more seriously about the future, I can anticipate that I'll regret having had the second drink soon after it is consumed. And I will regret it for every time afterward. I will prefer I'd abstained. I'm not drunk, nor am I overcome by emotions. What should I do?

There is nothing inherently irrational about having two drinks with a friend and leaving your car in the garage. As my friends will tell you, I don't always abstain. And sometimes I am very happy with my decision, despite its consequences. Still, in this case, the fact that I will inevitably regret the decision to drink as soon as the event is concluded seems to be a good reason for preferring to abstain. Indeed, the psychologists working on self-control recommend such self-projection as a strategy for resisting temptation. To make rational plans, we have to think not just about what would satisfy us now, but also what we will think of our predicament out into the future. Hence Walter Mischel:

> To resist a temptation we have to cool it, distance it from the self, and make it abstract. To take the future into account, we have to heat it, make it imminent and vivid. To plan for the future, it helps to pre-live it at least briefly, to imagine the alternative possible scenarios as if they were unfolding in the present. This allows us to anticipate the consequences of our choices, letting ourselves both feel hot and think cool.[4]

We see this technique vividly at work in the Singaporean retirement plan advertisements. They humorously portray the preferences you will have in a way that makes the reasons to save just as "hot"—as emotionally salient—as your present reasons to spend. But you shouldn't just try to predict how you'll *feel* about your decisions in the future. After all, our emotions at particular times aren't always under our control, easy to predict, or reflective of our reasons. You should also try to forecast what you'll reasonably prefer about your past choices. You should ask yourself: will I still prefer the choices that got me here?

[4] Mischel (2014: 146).

6.4 Regrets, Affirmations, and Planning

I think such forecasting is a commendable strategy for deliberating about our preferences and then making decisions. But we need to get more precise, particularly because rational forecasting strategies can easily be confused with other, more problematic approaches to rational planning.

Let's define a *regret* as a preference that you had acted differently in the past. Don't confuse this sense of regret with the painful emotional state that sometimes accompanies such preferences. For instance, I regret that I didn't buy Apple Computer stock in the early 1990s, but I don't beat myself up about it. And don't confuse this sense of regret with the belief that you were irrational in the past. Given my limited knowledge of the stock market and my tender age, I was perfectly rational to spend my money on video games instead of Apple shares. As we'll see in the cases to come, we can have regretting preferences even without present emotional distress. And it is a live question whether some of these preference changes are irrational.

Regret in our sense is nothing more than a preference you have at one time to have acted otherwise at an earlier time. We can define some related notions as well. We can call a present preference that you have acted as you actually did in the past an *affirmation*. Affirmations are the mirror images of intentions—present preferences that you will act in a particular way in the future. And we can call a preference you have now to not act a certain way in the future a *foreswearing* preference.[5]

As we see in the stock market case, sometimes we form regrets because we get new information about the world. I prefer I had purchased Apple stock back when it was $38.00 a share rather than $107.00, but I lacked crucial information about the company's future. And hindsight isn't always 20/20; sometimes we form regrets because we *lose* information about the world. Last winter I preferred to store all of my birdseed in difficult-to-open containers, high on the shelf in my garage, rather than in easy-to-open containers within reach. I stored the seed this way because I'd seen mice near the garage, and I knew they'd infest the house if they found a food source. Come summer, I will have completely forgotten about the mouse threat. I'll regret making the birdseed so hard to access, because I'll have forgotten the reason for my initial preference.

[5] Foreswearing preferences will be especially relevant to the arguments in Chapter 9.

Sometimes we form regrets because we stop rationally responding to our reasons. Such was the case with Odysseus. In the *Odyssey*, he ties himself to the mast of his ship so he can hear the song of the Sirens but be prevented from joining them in the depths. As his ship approaches the Sirens, he begs to be untied. Driven mad by their songs, his previous reasons have no effect on his preferences. Likewise, we sometimes form regrets because we *gain* rational faculties. As a young child, I had a pathological fear of injections. At age five, my mother took me for the standard course of pre-kindergarten vaccinations. I had a meltdown in the doctor's office once I realized what was happening. I needed to be physically restrained. Afterward my mother attempted to reassure me by telling me that I would not need any more shots until I went to middle school. I recall for the next year or so wishing every night that I would die in my sleep before I turned eleven, so I wouldn't have to face such a horrible fate. In retrospect, I prefer not to have troubled myself (or my mother) with such preferences. And that is because I have a much cooler and rational approach to my health as an adult.

Which is all to say, our preferences very well may change when we gain or lose information or if we gain or lose rational faculties. But these kinds of preference change are not what is going on in the Second Drink case. When I am deliberating about what I prefer, I am not missing any relevant information. I am not drunk or crazy or at an immature stage of development. And I think the fact that I reasonably believe I will regret the second drink licenses me to abstain now.

This reasoning suggests a principle which I will call *Strong Forecasting*:

> **Strong Forecasting:** If you have and always will have all of the relevant information about the options available to you, then you ought to prefer any option you know you will never regret in favor of one you know you will eventually regret.

The "ought" here is the ought of prudential rationality. An option is a state of affairs that you can choose to make actual, like choosing to have a second drink. In the drinking case, Strong Forecasting entails that I ought to prefer to abstain, since I will never regret abstaining going forward, but I will regret having the drink. Having the relevant information also entails having the faculties that help you appreciate your reasons for your preferences.

You might think Strong Forecasting is too strong, since it requires always setting aside present preferences any time they are swamped by future ones. The bookstore buddhists of Chapter 2 might be offended because it prohibits sometimes living in the moment, future be damned. There is a weaker form of the principle that can accommodate the bookstore buddhists:

> **Weak Forecasting:** If you have and always will have all of the relevant information about the options available to you, then it is *permissible* for you to prefer any option you know you will never regret in favor of one you know you will eventually regret.

Weak Forecasting is consistent with Mischel's approach to resisting temptation, though it is *very weak*. It does not, for instance, say you must ever defer to your future interests. It only says that it is permissible. On another way of looking at it, your future preferences give you licensing reasons but not obligating reasons.

Rational reflection principles occur periodically in the literature on decision theory, especially as it pertains to addressing problems with temptation.[6] If you think prudential rationality is just a matter of satisfying your preferences, you face a problem noted by Plato, the Epicureans, and the utilitarians (among many others): should you just satisfy your present preferences? And the answer—endorsed by all of these figures—is that being prudentially rational does not require blind deference to your present preferences. You may take your anticipated preferences into account, and often it is a good idea. Otherwise, you are doomed to always take the second drink, and morning after morning wake up without your car.

Weak Forecasting is a principle for how to plan around anticipated preference change. It applies to cases where you have rational preference change without any change in your underlying reasons. So if you think temptation cases like the Second Drink are possible, you are committed

[6] Preston Greene and I defended Weak Forecasting in Greene and Sullivan (2015). Frank Arntzenius (2008: 277) endorses the following principle: "A rational person should not be able to foresee that she will regret her decisions." See also Nagel (1970b: Chapter 6), Rawls (1971: 421–3), and Loomes and Sugden (1982). Principles like Weak Forecasting can also be described in terms of preferences about how our preferences are satisfied. For instance, it is rationally permissible to prefer an option where all of your preferences are satisfied over one where only some are.

to a form of preference permissivism—the same total set of reasons can justify more than one set of rational preferences. Because I think such cases are possible (indeed, in the Second Drink case, actual), I resisted preference impermissivism back in Chapter 3.

There is a third principle in the vicinity that we might use to decide between options even when there is no "regret free" path:

> **Balanced Forecasting:** If you have and always will have all of the relevant information about the options available to you, then it is permissible for you to prefer any option you know you will mostly* never regret over any option you know you will mostly* regret.

In this case we can qualify "mostly" in stronger or weaker ways, depending on your threshold for allowing your future preferences to license choices. You might, for instance, think it is rationally permissible to prefer an option you'll only regret on Christmas over an option you'll regret every Monday morning. As it turns out, we only need the Weak Forecasting principle to run the arguments of this chapter, but we'll briefly return to this more flexible variant in Chapters 9 and 10 when we apply the same general strategy to other planning problems.[7]

6.5 The No Regrets Argument

We can use the Weak Forecasting principle to develop a second argument for past neutrality.[8] Like the Mixed Tradeoff Argument, it turns on the irrational tradeoffs that a past discounter will be willing to make. Begin by considering a somewhat fanciful example that will allow the logic of the argument to become more vivid:

> **Magic Marshmallows:** Magic marshmallows carry all of the pleasure of the very best normal marshmallows, but with none of the deleterious nutritional side effects. Indeed, consuming a magic marshmallow makes you very happy for a short period of time. And the more you

[7] Balanced Forecasting is more susceptible to infinitary paradoxes, where agents are asked to form preferences involving tradeoffs of infinite amounts of well-being for infinite amounts of suffering. See Arntzenius et al. (2004).

[8] I developed this argument with Preston Greene in Greene and Sullivan (2015). I am greatly indebted to Preston Greene and Tom Dougherty for discussion of these cases.

eat, the more happiness you enjoy for that short time. The local grocery store is offering free samples of magic marshmallows this week. If you go today, you can eat ten at once. If you wait until Friday, you will only get one.

What should you do? This should be a no-brainer. Ten magic marshmallows now would be much better than waiting for just one—you should prefer to have the marshmallows immediately.

But not so fast. Suppose you subscribe to Weak Forecasting and you are disposed to discount the past. You can give yourself the following argument as you are about to consume the ten marshmallows:

The Reverse Marshmallow Test

(1) Weak Forecasting is true.

(2) It is rationally permissible to absolutely discount past pleasures.

(3) You will never regret choosing to wait for fewer marshmallows, because you will discount the ten present marshmallows as soon as they are consumed.

(4) You will regret choosing to consume the ten present marshmallows, because there are times between now and Friday when you will prefer future marshmallows to past ones.

C. So you should prefer to choose waiting for fewer marshmallows over presently consuming more.

This argument—like Carrie's argument for extending her Crossfit—is absurd. Moreover, someone who formed preferences this way would fail to seize time-sensitive opportunities for gain, and her life would go worse for it. (If you don't think marshmallow consumption contributes to a life going well, just substitute in whatever more realistic, discountable good you think does.)

We can make this into a more general argument for past neutrality:

The No Regrets Argument

(1) Weak Forecasting is true.

(2) If absolute past discounting is rationally permissible, then it is rational to prefer a lesser, later good to a greater, present one.

(3) At any given time, a rational agent prefers that her life going forward go as well as possible. (The Success principle)

(4) To prefer lesser goods to greater ones is to prefer one's life not go as well as possible.

C. Absolute past discounting is not rationally permissible.

We assume the agent isn't near-biased (in line with the arguments in Chapters 1–4 of this book). We also assume that the probabilities of getting the various goods have already been determined and factored into the agent's valuing. And we assume that past discounting for pains and pleasures is absolute, though related puzzles can be raised for agents who employ non-absolute discount functions.[9]

Premise (2) follows from the way Weak Forecasting and absolute past discounting interact, as shown in the marshmallow example. Premises (3) and (4) carry over directly from the Life-Saving Argument in Chapter 2. The action, so to speak, is around Premise (1). I will end this chapter by defending Weak Forecasting against some potential objections.

6.6 The Dead Have No Regrets

You might think Weak Forecasting is too strong because it entails it is rationally permissible to commit suicide. Consider how it applies to the following example:

Precipice: You find yourself now at both a geological and an existential precipice. You could go on with your life, but you are certain that in going on, there are times in the future when you'll regret it. You could also throw yourself off the precipice, immediately ending your life. Should you prefer that your life end and on that basis take the leap?

You may use Weak Forecasting to offer yourself the following argument: "I'll never regret dying, since the dead have no preferences. I will sometimes regret not dying. So by Weak Forecasting, it is rationally permissible for me to kill myself."

Are applications like this a counterexample to Weak Forecasting? Some comments. First, strictly speaking Weak Forecasting does not apply to such a case, since in dying you lose access to your reasons and so fail to

[9] See Section IV of Greene and Sullivan (2015).

satisfy the antecedent. But that can easily be accommodated by adding an innocent qualification to the original principle:

> **Weak Forecasting***: If now and for every time you consciously exist, you have and will have all of the relevant information about your situation and the capacity to appreciate that information, then it is rationally permissible to prefer any option you will never regret over any option you will eventually regret.

This accommodates the fact that one of your options entails loss of reasons by loss of conscious existence.

Second, we might think that anyone contemplating suicide in a case like this is compromised in her faculties and not appreciating her reasons, and so Weak Forecasting is not applicable. But to make the case interesting, let's suppose that you are not overwhelmed with depression as you stand on the precipice. Instead you are looking towards your future in a sober and reasons-responsive way. Perhaps persuaded by Albert Camus, you have surveyed the absurdity of existence and judged that living your life is no longer worth the effort.

Even granting the suicidal their rational faculties, remember that Weak Forecasting is intended as a principle about prudential rationality. If you think there is a strong moral injunction against suicide, that moral injunction will act as a side constraint, providing non-prudential reasons that override your prudential reasons, and give you an all-things-considered reason not to jump. So for the Precipice case to be a problem for Weak Forecasting, it must be that we think jumping could not be licensed by reasons of self-interest.

To determine whether you'd be rational to jump, we will likely want still more information about the case. Will you always prefer you had died on the precipice? Or will these preferences be brief and fleeting? We could add to Weak Forecasting a further qualification to distinguish these cases:

> **Weak Forecasting for Life Extension**: If now and for every time you consciously exist, you have and will have all of the relevant information about your situation and the capacity to appreciate that information, then it is rationally permissible to prefer any option you will always affirm or be indifferent towards over an option that you will not always affirm or be indifferent towards (either because you will regret it or lack conscious existence).

This version of Weak Forecasting delivers the same problem for past discounting as regular Weak Forecasting, since a discounter will always either affirm or be indifferent towards the meager future good. But it delivers a better diagnosis in the Precipice case. If it turns out you will always prefer to have died or be indifferent to living, it may very well be rationally permissible to die (modulo all of the important moral and psychological qualifications raised above). But if you will sometimes prefer you'd lived going forward, then Weak Forecasting for Life Extension does not entail suicide is rationally permissible, since it does not apply to your case.

This reasoning will get trickier when we apply it to more complicated real-world cases of deciding to extend your life in the face of radical change. I'll tackle those issues separately in Chapter 10. For now, note that we can qualify Weak Forecasting to make it suicide-proof.

6.7 The Teen Pregnancy Problem

Elizabeth Harman thinks principles similar to Weak Forecasting deliver implausible verdicts especially in cases where deep personal attachments are involved. Discussing her arguments will help us get more clear on how to apply principles like Weak Forecasting.

Harman's target is a principle which she calls *Reflection for Desires*:

> **Reflection for Desires:** If a person reasonably believes that in the future she will reasonably prefer that p be true, and she reasonably believes that she won't be in a worse epistemic or evaluative position at that time, then she should now prefer that p be true.[10]

By "prefer" here, Harman just means having an all-things-considered desire.[11] Harman thinks we should reject Reflection for Desires because it implies that certain seemingly fallacious arguments are sound. For instance:

> **Family Planning (Harman):** Suppose that a fourteen-year-old girl is considering conceiving a child. She knows that she is very young, and that it will be easier for her to be a mother when she is older. She knows that if she has a child now, it will be much harder for her to get a good education; she may well have a less meaningful and fulfilling

[10] Harman (2009: 182). [11] Harman (2009: 184).

professional life if she conceives now. Nevertheless, she also knows that if she conceives now, she will raise a child whom she will love dearly. She will love him and be glad that he exists; she will not wish she had waited to conceive later in life. She reasons as follows:

1. If I conceive now, I will be glad I did it.
2. Therefore, I should conceive now.[12]

The teen's argument strikes us as absurd, but her inference would be licensed if Reflection for Desires were true. So Harman concludes that Reflection for Desires is false.

Reflection for Desires is stronger than Weak Forecasting, since it says that you *ought* to prefer now what you think you will prefer later. And unlike Weak Forecasting, Harman's reflection principle does not have the explicitly comparative clause—it doesn't say you must (or may) prefer regret-free paths *over* paths with certain regret. Harman later considers a somewhat weaker version of Reflection for Desires, one that claims only that it is reasonable to base your present desires on your anticipated future desires. She rejects that as well, because she thinks it is patently unreasonable for a fourteen-year-old to prefer to conceive.[13]

Reflection for Desires (and its weaker cousin) are *really* strong, and for these reasons Harman is right to question their plausibility. She goes on to diagnose the cases where Reflection for Desires is likely to backfire:

> Sometimes it is (or will be) reasonable to prefer an outcome even though the alternative would have been better (in all the ways one should care about). It is reasonable of deaf parents to prefer that an adult deaf child have come to be who she is, even though it would have been better (in all the ways they should care about) if their child had been cured of deafness. A teenager who has chosen to conceive will later be reasonable in preferring that her child exists, even though it would be better (in all the ways she should care about at the time she chooses) if she waits to conceive later.[14]

Harman also identifies an interesting "bootstrapping" problem for applying preference reflection principles to cases where deep attachments are involved. When attachments are involved, we are reasonable in preferring already existing states of affairs over merely possible ones, even when the merely possible ones *would have been better* had they come about.

[12] Harman (2009: 182). [13] Harman (2009: 190). [14] Harman (2009: 188).

Suppose you are deliberating about creating such an attachment. Before the attachment is created, you should prefer whatever would be best overall. But after the attachment is created, you should prefer whatever actually happened. This means taking your perfectly reasonable future preferences as a guide can lead you to unreasonably choose a worse state over a better one. More generally, we might suppose that there is an appropriate dependence relation that holds between reasons, preferences, and actions. An action (like conceiving) is rational at a time if it is based on a rational preference at that time. And a preference is rational at a time if it is properly based on reasons at that time. But in bootstrapping cases, the "reasons" depend upon the action being performed. Harman contends that attachment cases are one such example of illicit bootstrapping.

Do Harman's cases raise similar issues for Weak Forecasting? As noted, Weak Forecasting wouldn't apply to Harman's original family planning case, but it would apply to a similar one:

> **Family Planning (Weak Forecasting):** Lucy is a sexually active teenager, deliberating about her family planning preferences. Suppose she is entertaining two possibilities—become pregnant as soon as possible or have no children as a teenager. She knows that if she were to get pregnant tomorrow, she would deeply love her child. This deep love would lead her to always prefer that she'd had this particular pregnancy and this particular child. Because of this powerful love, she predicts she will never regret the pregnancy. She also knows that if she were to wait, she might occasionally prefer she'd had the child (especially when she spends time with friends' children). But she'd mostly prefer to have her current childless life or be indifferent.

In this case, Weak Forecasting entails it is rationally permissible to have the child. As with the suicide case, I think this is an example where compelling moral considerations are likely to affect our judgment. We might credibly think that it is always wrong for any fourteen-year-old to become a parent in this situation. Or we might think she is violating a duty to her future child in conceiving it while she is still so young. Or we might think that there are more heavy-handed principles for human flourishing which speak against teen pregnancy, whatever else the teen's interests are. For instance we might think we are always required to prioritize educational and career developments over parenthood. These are not problems for Weak Forecasting insofar as it is a principle of prudential rationality. Weak Forecasting requires being aware of all of the relevant reasons. If we think there is always a compelling reason to not conceive as a teen, she shouldn't prefer to conceive.

But suppose there is no absolute prohibition on becoming a teen parent. Do we still think it is also against Lucy's self-interest to prefer parenthood? Once we've screened out the moral considerations, it is not clear it is. To see why, consider a parallel case that does not have the same moral noise as the teen pregnancy case:

> **Family Planning (Without Conception):** Lucy is a teenager who grew up estranged from her grandparents. She is deliberating about whether to initiate a relationship with them. Suppose she is entertaining two possibilities—start a relationship or maintain the status quo. She knows that if she were to initiate a relationship, she would deeply love her grandparents. This deep love would lead her to always prefer that she'd had this particular relationship. She'd never regret it. She also knows that were she to maintain the status quo, she might occasionally prefer that she knew her grandparents. But she'd mostly prefer to have her current life, made rich with all of its current relationships.

If Lucy argues from Weak Forecasting to the conclusion that it is rationally permissible to start a relationship with her grandparents, do we think she is engaged in any kind of questionable bootstrapping? Again, I think not. But this case is exactly analogous to the second family planning case as a case of prudential rationality. Harman thinks that attachments generate reasons after the choice that simply could not be anticipated and weighed before the choice. If this is correct, then principles like Weak Forecasting would not apply to such plans, because they would essentially involve new information. But we also might reasonably think that we can forecast our preferences for anticipated attachments, and on these grounds, Lucy would be licensed to pursue the new relationship with her grandparents. What is misleading about the conception case, I'd argue, is our difficulty in thinking about the creation of human life in purely prudential terms. In any event, I think the Weak Forecasting principle for self-interested planning is immune from the bootstrapping objection that undoes stronger reflection principles.

6.8 Success and Neutrality

One of the most powerful arguments for future neutrality—the Life-Saving Argument—focuses on how temporal discounting can lead to imprudent future tradeoffs. As we've seen, there are parallel arguments—the Mixed Tradeoff Argument and the No Regrets Argument—which use similar considerations to defend past neutrality. I have argued that we are permitted to take our anticipated future preferences as reasons for forming our present preferences. Indeed, this is a good strategy for resisting near bias, and without such a strategy we'd have a difficult time forming and sticking to rational plans in the face of temptation. But if you discount the past, you will also be disposed to prefer tradeoffs that are clearly worse for you. So you should not discount the past.

Having found one way to defend past neutrality, let's now turn our attention to the other, which parallels the Arbitrariness Argument for Future Neutrality.

7

The Arbitrariness Argument (Again)

> If anyone pities the dead, he must also pity those who have not yet been born.
>
> Seneca the Younger, *Of Consolation, To Marcia*

7.1 Einstein's Hollow Condolences

Michele Angelo Besso and Albert Einstein first met while young students in Zurich. Years later Besso helped Einstein secure his job at the Swiss patent office. The two were fast friends, united by interests in physics and engineering. In 1905 one of the seemingly nondescript patent clerks wrote a series of short papers that revolutionized our understanding of space, time, and energy. And even as Einstein catapulted to fame and prestigious academic appointments, he maintained an intimate correspondence with Besso back in the patent office. On the occasion of Besso's death (and aware that he was nearing his own), Einstein wrote a letter of condolence to Besso's widow, Anna Winteler: "Now (Michele) has departed from this strange world a little ahead of me. That signifies nothing. For those of us who believe in physics, the distinction between past, present and future is only a stubbornly persistent illusion."[1]

What did Einstein mean? On one view of time—the B-theory of time—Besso's death did not terminate his existence. According to the B-theory, space and time and everything in it are spread out in a single manifold. The distinction between the past, present, and future is only intelligible

[1] Isaacson (2007: 540). Thanks to Jonah Shupbach for introducing me to the Einstein–Besso letters.

relative to particular observers in this manifold. According to the B-theorists, Besso still exists, albeit in the part of the manifold that we consider the past relative to our present location. It is as though his life is happening "over there," but not completely gone. The B-theory is often taken to be a consequence of Einstein's theory of Special Relativity.[2]

It is unclear what effect, if any, Einstein's letter of condolence had on Besso's grieving widow. Still I suspect that many of us, regardless of our interpretation of the theory of relativity, find the condolences somewhat . . . hollow. It doesn't matter if our loved ones are still "around" in some part of a vast spread-out space-time manifold—if that part is entirely in what we consider our past, then it is just as bad as if they had been annihilated. What explains this?

Perhaps what bothers us is that even if Einstein is right, we cannot interact with anyone who exists merely in our past. At most we have meaningful causal powers over events that are in our future, and only then over things that we could get to at a speed slower than the speed of light (another lesson from Special Relativity). But curiously we don't have a similar view about people in our present or future with whom we cannot—for all practical purposes—interact. We do not mourn now for our yet-to-be-born future descendants. And it isn't as though we treat loved ones who move far out of contact as though they are dead, however hyperbolic you might be at the going-away party. So when and why do we care about causal control?

Another potential explanation is that it is just a brute fact that something (a person, a life) being in the past makes it far less valuable. And so we prefer the lives of our loved ones to be occurring in the present and future and not to have faded into our past. Which raises another question: *should* rational agents be sensitive to whether events are past, present, or future?

The Epicureans did not have a theory of relativity, but they shared Einstein's intuition that the past/present/future distinction is no good

[2] In brief: Special Relativity hypothesizes a Minkowski geometry for space-time in order to explain the constant speed of light. In this structure, there is no way to distinguish a unique, absolute relation of simultaneity. And so there is no way to distinguish a unique, absolute present. So, the reasoning goes, the simplest explanation is that the only objectively real temporal relations are earlier/later-than relations. This is a controversial issue in the metaphysics of time. For an overview of the problem and a suggestion for how we might recover presentness in the theory of Special Relativity, see Skow (2015).

basis for forming preferences. As discussed in Chapter 3, the Epicureans were concerned with developing the appropriate attitudes towards time and pleasure. They were also concerned with appropriately responding to emotions, in particular emotions involving the most profound event any of us will ever consider—death. If you are anything like me, you are afraid of *how* you will die. Will it be painful? Sudden? Will you change dramatically in the process? But many of us are also, I suspect, dismayed at the prospect that there will be some time in the future (hopefully a long ways off) when we simply do not exist. Our loved ones will go on without us, and the world will continue to develop, but we will no longer be a character in the story. On this account—sometimes called the *deprivation account*—we can explain fear of death as the ultimate manifestation of fear of missing out.[3]

In his epic poem, *De Rerum Natura*, the Epicurean philosopher Lucretius offers therapy for this existential fear by asking his reader whether these attitudes are objectionably arbitrary: "Look back similarly at how the stretch of unending time before we are born has been nothing to us. Nature, therefore, offers this reflection to us of the time to come after our eventual death."[4] Ask yourself if you prefer to have been born significantly earlier. There were large segments of history where you were not interacting with any loved ones, not part of the developing story of the world, and not having adventures or conscious experiences. Most of us, when we reflect on this, are left cold. We certainly do not have a strong preference that we had lived any extra segments of life in the past. But, Lucretius urges, the period of past history we missed out on is not in any important way different from the period of history we will miss out on after our deaths. Our preferences about the past "hold up a mirror" showing us that there is nothing worth fretting about when it comes to the future. Once you realize this, you ought to rest satisfied with the life you have and not prefer that it be extended.

As with Einstein's attempt at condolence, most readers are skeptical of the Lucretian therapy. And there is a similar explanation for why we do not wake in a cold sweat contemplating the fact that we once did not exist. Those potential times would be *in the past*. And events in the past just matter far less—perhaps not even at all—compared with

[3] For discussion see Nagel (1970a).
[4] *De Rerum Natura* 3.972–3.975. The translation is from Warren (2004).

events in the future. But while we might be psychologically disposed to care less about the past, is this attitude justified? In this chapter, I will defend the Lucretian therapy by extending the Arbitrariness Argument for Future Neutrality we built in Chapters 3 and 4. The next section will describe an arbitrariness argument for past neutrality that results from straightforward amendments to its future-looking counterpart. The remainder of the chapter will consider and reject various candidates for a normatively significant difference between the past and future.[5]

7.2 The Arbitrariness Argument (Again)

Recall the Arbitrariness Argument for Future Neutrality (advanced by the Epicureans, Sidgwick, and others):

The Arbitrariness Argument for Future Neutrality

(1) At any given time, a prudentially rational agent's preferences are insensitive to arbitrary differences.
(2) Relative distance from the present is an arbitrary difference between events.
(3) If you are near-biased, your preferences are sensitive to when an event is scheduled relative to the present.
C. So at any given time, near-biased preferences are not rationally permissible.

As we saw in Chapter 3, the first premise derives its plausibility from considerations about what makes a particular preference an objectionable bias. By amending the second and third premises, we can construct a parallel argument for past neutrality:

The Arbitrariness Argument for Past Neutrality

(1) At any given time, a prudentially rational agent's preferences are insensitive to arbitrary differences.
(2) Being past rather than future is an arbitrary difference between events.
(3) If you are future-biased, your preferences are sensitive to when an event is scheduled relative to the present.

[5] Parts of this chapter are excerpted from Finochiarro and Sullivan (2016). And I am grateful to Peter Finocchiaro for extensive discussion of these points.

C. So at any given time, future-biased preferences are not rationally permissible.

I won't repeat the defense of Premise (1) (see Chapter 3). Premise (3) simply follows from what it is to be future-biased. The philosophical action centers around Premise (2). Is there any rationally significant difference between the properties of being past or being future? As we've seen in earlier chapters, we can intuitively sort properties into categories based on whether they supply reasons to back preferences. Probabilities are non-arbitrary. It is non-arbitrary whether some sacrifice will eventually be compensated, how much pleasure a certain good will give you, the quality of that pleasure, and (perhaps) how it fits structurally in your life. It is, however, arbitrary whether some pain will happen on a Tuesday, whether a sacrifice is described to you in terms of gains or losses, or whether some potential good is located to your left or to your right (assuming each is equally accessible). So another way of asking the Epicurean question is—where does the past/future distinction lie in this categorization? Is there any reason to think that it falls on the normatively significant end of the spectrum?

7.3 The Obvious Asymmetry

Consider a seemingly mundane case of future bias:

Colonoscopy: You are scheduled to have a routine but unpleasant colonoscopy next week. You prefer that the colonoscopy had already occurred.

Assume the colonoscopy is certain to happen. Is there a non-arbitrary difference between a certain routine colonoscopy that is scheduled a week from now and a routine colonoscopy that has already occurred?

One candidate immediately suggests itself: the difference between past and future colonoscopies is that one has the property of *being past* and the other has the property of *being future*. These differences *by themselves* are normatively significant. And its being past is always a reason to discount an event. Call this the *obvious defense* of future bias.[6]

There are two difficulties with the obvious defense. First, it pressures supporters to take a stand in a fraught debate in the metaphysics of time.

[6] See discussion in Finochiarro and Sullivan (2016).

According to so-called "A-theories" of time, the properties of *being past* and *being future* are intrinsic and irreducible properties of times and events.[7] In contrast, the "B-theories" of time (like Einstein's) hold that these properties are reducible to locations in a space-time manifold.[8] A B-theorist who wants to maintain the obvious defense seems to be saddled with an inconsistent triad of views. First, most of us think it is irrational to discriminate merely on the basis of locational properties. For instance, the mere fact that a brand of detergent is stocked at eye level is no reason to pay more for it than one stocked just lower, if both are easily accessible and similarly effective. (See Section 3.2.) Second, the obvious defense claims that it is rational to discriminate merely on the basis of tensed properties. Third, the B-theorist thinks that tensed properties are reducible to locational properties in a space-time manifold. So it is hard to see how the B-theorist could maintain that these temporal properties are rationally significant in a way that locational properties are not while simultaneously claiming that temporal properties are nothing over and above locational properties.[9] And even if the B-theorist is able to do this, it is clear that the metaphysical questions at play cannot be sidestepped. So pushing the obvious defense forces us into tricky debates about the nature of temporal properties, raising doubts about its obviousness.

That said, I am an A-theorist. If, like me, you have firmly held metaphysical grounds for supporting the A-theory, should you be more sympathetic with the obvious defense of future bias? I think not, because there are cases where merely *being past* does not provide reason to discount. For instance, as we saw with Hurka's Discoveries case in Chapter 5, its being in the past does not seem to make an achievement any less valuable. So the defender of future bias also owes us a theory for why being in the past is normatively significant when applied to pains and pleasures

[7] Examples of various kinds of A-theories include Broad (1923), Prior (1967), Adams (1989), Zimmerman (1998), Crisp (2003), Markosian (2004), Forrest (2006), Merricks (2007), and Sullivan (2012b).

[8] Examples of B-theories include Russell (1915), Quine (1950), Lewis (1986), Price (1996), and Sider (2001).

[9] A suggestion: the B-theorist might argue that the analogy between space and space-time should not be taken as strongly as it is here. Location in the space-time manifold is fundamentally different than ordinary spatial location. Therefore, the fact that ordinary location bias is irrational has no bearing on the rationality of space-time bias. This suggestion requires the B-theorist to offer a theory of space-time location that explains the disanology.

but not when applied to other sorts of events. The temporal property by itself does not automatically provide a reason to discount.

There are other asymmetries associated with the past and future. For instance, we commonly think the future is potentially within our control while the past is not (barring the possibility of time travel). The future is open while the past is necessary. We tend to be more attached to our *actual* pasts than ways our pasts could have gone. And our emotions are more sensitive to the future than the past. Could any of these asymmetries provide a non-arbitrary basis for future bias? Let's consider each in turn.

7.4 The Asymmetry of Emotion

One way defenders of future bias might try to justify having asymmetric preferences towards the past and future is by appealing to asymmetries in our emotions about our past and future. As a matter of psychology, we are emotionally disposed to care more about experiences in our future than experiences in our past. We typically experience pleasure now anticipating future pleasures but far less remembering past ones. We experience pain now dreading future pains but have comparatively little concern for past ones. This asymmetry makes good evolutionary sense—it focuses our attention on securing pleasures and avoiding pains that might be under our control. According to the *emotion defense*, we are justified in discounting the past because we have temporally asymmetric emotions.

Any adequate theory of rational planning should take into account anticipated emotions and the ways in which these emotions affect our well-being. For instance, if you know you are bound to experience dread before the colonoscopy and you know you can dull this emotion by taking a Valium now, you might rationally prefer to take the drug now. Nevertheless we need to distinguish two attitudes you could take towards these emotions. First you can factor your present or anticipated emotions into your rational planning, as in the Valium-before-colonoscopy example. This is perfectly justified. Second, you can take your different emotions regarding past and future events as independent reasons to be rationally concerned with properties like *being past* and *being future*. This is unjustified. We have similarly powerful temporally asymmetric emotions in the case of near bias. I dread tomorrow's colonoscopy but don't give a second thought to next year's procedure. I'd be relieved to discover my colonoscopy has been postponed a year. These emotions aren't taken as evidence that near bias is rational—they are just psychological facts about how our present emotions are sensitive to beliefs about time.

There is a lot more to say about the relationship between our emotions and our time biases, but I will reserve those issues for the next chapter. For now, note that the temporal asymmetry of emotions won't answer the arbitrariness charge against past discounting any more than the asymmetry of emotions could answer the same charge against distant future discounting.

7.5 The Asymmetry of Attachment

Does it matter that we tend to be more attached to the actual past than we do to merely possible ways the past could have gone or merely possible ways the future could go? In the last chapter, we saw Elizabeth Harman claim that we are tempted into bad "I'll be glad I did it" arguments because we have a perfectly justifiable attachment to actual past events. She writes, "Sometimes it is (or will be) reasonable to prefer an outcome even though the alternative would have been better (in all the ways one should care about) . . . A teenager who has chosen to conceive will later be reasonable in preferring that her child exists, even though it would be better (in all the ways she should care about at the time she chooses) if she waits to conceive later."[10] Or consider another case, used by Robert Adams to defend a similar principle:

> **Helen Keller:** Would it have been reasonable for Helen Keller, as an adult, to wish, for her own sake, that she had never been blind or deaf? I think not. Let us suppose that she would have had an even better and happier life if her sight and hearing had been spared (though that is not obviously true). But whatever its excellences, that life would not have had one day in it that would have been very like any day of her actual life after the age of 19 months. Her actual life—in its emotional as well as its sensory qualities, in its skills and projects, and doubtless in much of her personality and character—was built around the fact of her blindness and deafness . . . Her never having been blind or deaf would have been

[10] Harman (2009: 188).

> very like her never having existed. Why should she wish for that, given that she had reason to be glad she existed?[11]

Adams then generalizes: "If our lives are good, we have the same sort of reason to be glad we have had them rather than lives that would have been even better but too thoroughly different, as we have to be glad that we exist and not better and happier people instead of us." We can call this the *conservation constraint* on preferences: an agent is sometimes rational in preferring some possible past events over others because they actually happened, even if they are less valuable than other merely possible events. Could the conservation constraint help block Premise (2) of the Arbitrariness Argument for Past Neutrality? Maybe because we are often justified in preferring our actual past, we are likewise often justified in absolutely discounting counterfactual past pains and pleasures, since if they'd happened, then the actual past events wouldn't have. For example, like many others, as a child I had braces. I suffered three years of painful teeth-straightening with metal brackets, wires, and the like. If I'd waited until the present to work on my teeth, I could have had the same procedure with far less suffering by using invisible, custom-fitted plastic teeth straighteners. But perhaps I prefer to have had the past pain, since the experience of overcoming that suffering as a youth made me into the resilient adult I am today. Can such reasoning be deployed in any systematic way to justify past discounting?

I am not sure what to make of the cases that attempt to justify the conservation constraint. For example, it isn't *obvious* that Helen Keller is prudentially rational in preferring she be deaf and blind. But even if we grant the conservation constraint, it is not strong enough to justify past discounting. For one, it won't explain why it is ever rational to prefer merely possible past pains to potential future ones. Suppose I never had braces as a child, but I am asked whether I prefer to have had the painful metal treatment as a child or to have the less painful plastic treatment now as an adult. If I am a past discounter, presumably I'll prefer to have already had my teeth straightened, however unpleasantly. But this preference couldn't be explained by any attachment to the actual past.

Moreover, the vast majority of past pains and pleasures are not essential to the process by which we became who we are. As a matter of actual

[11] Adams (1979: 60).

autobiography, I do not think having braces as a child played a role in my settled adult personality. I don't know many people who associate their deepest present attachments with past pains and pleasures attachment value (if there is such value) is characteristically non-hedonic. So the value of attachments is not going to supply any good grounds for hedonic past discounting, the most prevalent form of discounting.

7.6 The Asymmetry of Control

We've looked at emotional and attachment-based differences between the past and future, but neither were strong enough to block the Arbitrariness Argument. Maybe we should look instead to the metaphysical differences between the past and future to find a normatively significant asymmetry. We have yet to discover a way to travel backward in time, so events in the past are settled and outside of your control. But many future events are unsettled and potentially within your control. For instance, you have no control now over whether particular painful medical procedures *already* happened to you. But you do have control now over whether you show up for the colonoscopy.

In Chapter 5 we considered and rejected the control constraint on preferences. Recall that the control constraint held that only preferences over events within an agent's control could be judged as rational or irrational. The control constraint was both too restrictive (it ruled out weather preferences) and too permissive (it permitted you to be money pumped). But we could reject the control constraint and still assume that it is rational to care less about events that are beyond your control and so rational to discount past events. The defender of future bias might offer an argument along these lines:

The Control Argument for Non-Arbitrariness

(1) Any past pain or pleasure is (now) certainly beyond your control.
(2) It is rationally permissible to discount events that are not within your control.
C. So it is rationally permissible to discount past pleasures and pains.

The trouble with this defense of future bias is Premise (2)—control discounting is not rationally permissible. Suppose you are asked your preference over two potential future windfalls. In one future, you'll be offered the chance to do an easy task (which you can accept or reject) that will give you an hour of pleasure. In another future, you'll be simply overcome with joy and as a result have two hours of pleasure. It is perfectly rational to prefer the future windfall over which you have no control to the one in which you exercise control, especially if both options have no consequences for your life afterward. Indeed, it would be bizarre to apply an *absolute* discount function to events just because they are beyond your control, which is what a control defense of absolute past discounting would require. Control might matter significantly to our moral assessment of agents—we might find you more deserving if you earn your fortune by honest toil.[12] And feelings of control might tend to contribute to our feelings of pride and motivation at a time, especially when it applies to challenging activities.[13] But lack of control is no reason to systematically discount events.

7.7 The Asymmetry of Possibility

You might still think the "settledness" of the past provides a non-arbitrary reason to discount. For instance, perhaps it is always rational to prefer an impossible pain to a possible one. Because you did not have a colonoscopy yesterday, your past colonoscopy is impossible. And so it is rational to prefer the past pain (effectively discounting it). Likewise, in the case of pleasures, perhaps it is always rational to prefer a possible pleasure over an impossible one. Let's switch from colonoscopies to a more pleasurable activity: aromatherapy massages. Suppose you are asked whether you prefer to have had an hour-long massage yesterday or to be scheduled for a (certain) one tomorrow. You may argue that you prefer the future massage because it is metaphysically possible, whereas it is impossible that you had a massage yesterday. The past is settled and as a matter of necessity it includes no massage. Should the necessity of the past make a difference for rational preferences?

We can make these suggestions into a more general argument:

The Modal Argument for Non-Arbitrariness

(1) It is (now) impossible that the past be any other way than it actually is.

[12] Nagel (1979). [13] Duhigg (2016: Chapter 1).

(2) Any merely future event is (now) possible.

(3) It is rationally permissible to prefer a possible pleasure to any impossible pleasure.

(4) It is rationally permissible to prefer any impossible pain to any possible pain.

C. So it is rationally permissible to discount past pleasures and pains.

Here the relevant sense of "necessity" and "possibility" is broadly metaphysical rather than epistemic or conceptual. We are meant to read Premise (1) as saying there is no possible world where the past is different but the actual present is the same.

As stated, the Modal Argument for Non-Arbitrariness is logically invalid. Premises (1)–(4) only entail that it is rationally permissible to discount past pleasures and pains *that did not already occur*. Suppose I had an unpleasant but routine colonoscopy yesterday. It lasted twenty minutes. The doctor informs me today that if I'd waited to have it tomorrow, she could have used a new probe and finished the procedure in just ten minutes. I prefer the longer actual past colonoscopy to any shorter future one. Premises (1)–(4) are silent on whether past discounting for actual events is rationally permissible. To handle cases like this, we would need to strengthen Premise (4) to any impossible *or* any necessary pain (like my actual, necessary past colonoscopy). But that's absurd. Any metaphysically necessary event is also a metaphysically possible one, so the revised premise is incoherent.[14]

The Modal Argument for Non-Arbitrariness is no good. But maybe modal constraints can pose more direct problems for past neutrality. You might, for instance, think that rationality requires all agents to assign zero probability to any metaphysically impossible state of affairs—no other subjective probability is rationally permissible. This may be because you think probabilities must be defined over a space of metaphysically possible worlds. Or it may be because you think probabilities must accord with evidence and all evidence tells against a metaphysical impossibility ever coming to be. If you think rationality requires assigning zero probability to any impossible state of affairs, and you think a state of affairs must have some positive probability to be thought of as a news item over

[14] At least in modal logics as strong as D. As a matter of course, most philosophers assume stronger logics for metaphysical modality.

which rational preferences range, then you might think you must never rationally prefer an impossibility to a good possibility. We can call this the *modal constraint* on preferences. The modal constraint would generate problems for past neutrality, since past neutrality requires indifference about whether pleasures are yet to occur or, *per impossibile*, have already occurred.[15]

This certainly won't be a direct or uncontroversial objection to past neutrality. Many decision theorists, for instance, find it natural to construct subjective utilities and subjective probabilities by taking preferences as basic.[16] But this argument for the modal constraint puts matters the other way around. Moreover, a modal constraint on preferences seems to rule out some perfectly coherent and psychologically realistic preferences. Consider the following case:

> **Party Game:** Ryan and Ruth are playing a party game called "Would you rather . . ." Ryan asks Ruth who she'd rather be: Michelle Obama or Melania Trump. Ruth says she would prefer to be Obama, since Obama is more eloquent and professionally accomplished.

On most views of metaphysical necessity, it is metaphysically impossible for Ruth to be either Obama or Trump. So the modal constraint entails that the only rational preference Ruth can have in the Party Game is indifference. But this is far too restrictive. It is rationally permissible to prefer to be Obama, especially given Ruth's reasons.

Defenders of future bias might worry that we've misrepresented the Party Game case. When Ruth claims that she would prefer to be Michelle Obama, all she means is that she would prefer to have Michelle Obama's most salient properties: being First Lady, being an intelligent and accomplished leader, having wit and grace, etc. It is possible for her to instantiate *these* properties. On this approach, when someone claims to have a preference about a metaphysical impossibility, charity dictates that we interpret that preference as being over the most similar metaphysically possible state of affairs. If we take such a position on attitudes

[15] Jeffrey (1983) contends that preferences over states of affairs with zero probability are undefined, so he would not endorse the Modal Argument. But there is reason to think Jeffrey's approach is too restrictive; see Nolan (2006).

[16] See Buchak (Forthcoming).

towards impossible worlds, then the modal constraint starts to look more viable.

Still, you might think that this charity is misguided in the Party Game case. Perhaps Ruth really doesn't want to be like Obama—she wants to be Obama. She wants the essence of Obama. The defender of the modal constraint must insist that this preference is irrational. And there are other cases where this strategy more obviously won't help. Consider:

> **Resurrection:** Suppose persons just are their bodies, and if death and decomposition occur, then it is impossible that a person be resurrected. Suppose Mike knows this, and Mike is afraid of death. Mary asks if Mike would prefer to be resurrected from the dead in a hundred years or prefer that a person similar to Mike now, with similar quasi-memories and similar psychological dispositions, be brought into existence. Mike says he would prefer for purely self-interested reasons that *he* be resurrected. He wants more life.

The modal constraint dictates that Mike cannot rationally prefer his resurrection (since that is impossible). But again, this result seems unjustifiably restrictive. Mike's preference to be resurrected is rationally permissible. In a less eschatological way, we might be unsure of our persistence conditions over long intervals and radical change. But worrying about whether our persistence over such intervals is metaphysically impossible does not prevent us from forming rationally evaluable long-run preferences for lives.

One more case makes the point, this one drawn from history. Enlightenment-era philosopher Thomas Hobbes got himself into a bit of trouble when he claimed in his 1656 book *De Corpore* that he'd discovered a proof of how to square a circle. His academic arch-nemesis John Wallis published an essay accusing Hobbes of mathematical inconsistency and carelessness. The controversy took its toll on Hobbes's career, and he preferred that he had discovered an incontrovertible proof of how to square the circle, in order to rehabilitate his reputation and give Wallis his comeuppance. Of course, no such proof is possible. But Hobbes had self-interested reasons to prefer that the impossible occur.

The modal constraint—like the control constraint—is too restrictive. But without the modal constraint, it is hard to see how the settledness of the past could provide a good basis for past discounting.

7.8 Non-Arbitrariness and Neutrality

We've looked at five potential ways of getting out of the Arbitrariness Argument for Past Neutrality, but none of the routes withstood scrutiny. The past/future distinction seems just as rationally arbitrary as the near/distant distinction, even if it has more promise for being an important metaphysical distinction. So with the original Arbitrariness Argument of Chapters 3 and 4, we now seem to have a unified case for rationality requiring temporal neutrality. To the extent that you agree that rationality requires preferences be suitably grounded in reasons, you shouldn't discount the past or the future.

Does this mean we are obliged to accept Einstein and Lucretius' indifference to death? Of course not—you can be temporally neutral and still prefer that you and your loved ones have more good life rather than less. You should just be indifferent as to when that good life occurs. How weird is it to approach your life with a temporally neutral stance? This is the topic of our remaining four chapters.

8

Understanding Temporal Neutrality

> Others mistrust and say, "But time escapes: Live now or never!"
> He said, "What's time? Leave Now for the dogs and the apes! Man has forever."
>
> Robert Browning, *A Grammarian's Funeral*

In the preceding chapters I have offered a case for two general claims:

1. We should treat near bias and future bias similarly. Both can be understood as preferences for when events are scheduled (or would be scheduled) in our lives. The same rational considerations can be brought to bear on both kinds of preferences. And they are preferences that can and should be studied in a more unified and systematic way by social scientists.
2. There are plausible philosophical arguments for thinking that both near bias and future bias are irrational.

But if these time biases are irrational, then why do we have them? And what would it mean to be temporally neutral? These questions guide the last part of this book.

In this chapter, I will explain what a temporally neutral approach to rational planning does—and, perhaps more importantly, doesn't—require of us. And I will offer an account of why our time biases, though irrational, are so persistent.

I do not want to just offer a general theory of prudential rationality in this book. As I mentioned in the introduction, I think a theory of prudential rationality should be judged in part by its fruits—can it guide our approach to planning problems that we otherwise have a difficult time deliberating about? In the final three chapters I will take up these applications. I'll consider when it is rational to stick to your plans, even if you've changed your mind. I'll offer a theory of when you can prefer your life go on even in the face of a radical change, like becoming quadriplegic or developing Alzheimer's disease. I'll also offer a theory of how temporally neutral agents reason about the value of an afterlife. And I'll consider how temporal neutrality justifies the ways we assign meaning to projects we pursue.

But first, the general theory of temporal neutrality.

8.1 A Perceptual Model for Past Discounting?

If the arguments from previous chapters are convincing, then we are disposed to discount the past and future but such systematic discounting is irrational. Any time a theory postulates widespread irrationality, it owes us a theory of error: an explanation for why we mistakenly take a set of preferences, beliefs, or actions as rational. One option is to just think our discounting tendencies are basic components of our psychology, a feature of our valuing that is not susceptible of any further explanation. This may have been Bentham's view on future discounting (hence his willingness to include propinquity as a variable in the hedonic calculus).[1] But this hypothesis is unsatisfying both because it does not offer anything by way of philosophical explanation nor does it suggest any ways we could move forward in measuring and correcting our time biases.

A more sophisticated theory of error for future discounting comes from Plato. Recall from Chapter 2, in the *Protagoras* Plato recommends learning the "art of measurement" as a strategy for making correct now-for-later tradeoffs. In the same passage, Plato offers a theory for why this art of measurement is a necessary corrective to our natural planning tendencies:

> Do things of the same size appear to you larger when seen near at hand and smaller when seen from a distance? . . . If, then, our well-being depended upon this doing and choosing large things, avoiding and not doing the small ones, what would we see as our salvation in life? . . . The art of measurement . . . would make appearances lose their power . . . (356c–e)

[1] See Section 3.1.

Plato leans on a measurement analogy—as something is moved further away, it appears smaller and so its true size is obscured by its appearance. We can call this the *perceptual model* for future discounting.[2] On this model, future discounting is a kind of error in belief. As events are scheduled into the more distant future, they incorrectly appear as though they would contribute less value or disvalue to our lives.

The perceptual model of near bias was controversial even in the fifth century BCE. It figures prominently in Socrates' famous denial of the possibility of weakness of will. And like any of these models, it is subject to verification from empirical work in psychology. If the perceptual model for near bias were correct, then demonstrating the correct value of a distant event ought to diminish our discount rates. For instance, correctly calculating the growth from compound interest ought to spur increased retirement saving. Explaining the predictable symptoms of type 2 diabetes should increase dieting behavior. But there is little evidence that such strategies alone successfully reduce discount rates.[3]

Moreover, the perceptual model predicts that there would be no significant difference between how we discount self-interestedly and how we discount the value of events for others we are concerned about. For instance, suppose I'm consulted about whether *you* should forgo a vacation this year in order to make a significant deposit in your retirement account. The perceptual model predicts I'd have the same saving preference for you as I would for myself in a similar tradeoff; if it is mere temporal distance that predicts discounting, then your value on the distant horizon is subject to the same magnitude illusion as my own. This is a prediction that could be tested empirically (though as far as I can tell, it has not been). As we'll see in the next section, there is evidence of some robust self/other asymmetries in our discounting attitudes.[4]

Further, the perceptual model does not offer a plausible model of past discounting. On the perceptual model, presumably past discounting would be explained as a systematic defect in our memories. We remember pains as significantly better than they in fact were and pleasures as

[2] The model also appears in *Philebus* 41e9–42c4.

[3] There is evidence that promoting certain methods of deliberation on reasons decreases discount rates; see Weber et al. (2007). For discussion of the role of emotion and empathy in building complementary models, see Hershfield et al. (2011).

[4] See Hare (2008) for philosophical discussion. There is evidence we discount future selves at similar rates as we discount the interests of others. See Pronin et al. (2008).

significantly worse than they were. While our memories certainly exhibit valuing biases, there is little empirical support for thinking memory has *this kind* of bias.[5] And the perceptual model could not explain our tendency to abruptly and absolutely discount recent pains and pleasures—presumably events we still have reliable memories of.

We should look for a different explanation of our temporal discounting, ideally one that can offer a unified theory of error for our time biases. In the next two sections, I will develop this alternative, which we might call the *evolved emotional heuristic* model for temporal discounting. The model predicts a robust self/other asymmetry in our time biases, driven by the role that temporally asymmetric emotions play in our preference formation. It also predicts that time biases are advantageous in simple planning frameworks, since temporal properties can serve as useful heuristics for probability and control. To develop the model, we should first consider some additional empirical descriptions of our time biases.

8.2 Self and Other Asymmetries

Remember the Caruso, Gilbert, and Wilson study from back in Chapter 5? They measured past discounting indirectly by measuring how our views of appropriate compensation change if we've already completed a boring job (versus still having to complete it). They found that we are likely to ask for far less compensation if a boring job is over and done with.

But what happens when we are asked to form a preference about how much *someone else* should be paid for a boring job? Are we still disposed to discount someone else's pain if it is already over? Caruso, Gilbert, and Wilson set out to find an answer. Here is what they found:

> **My Boring Job vs. Someone Else's:** One hundred eighty-two people from a study pool in Boston read a version of the [boring data entry] story. Some participants (self-relevant condition) were asked to imagine that they would do (or had done) the work, and others (self-irrelevant condition) were asked to imagine that a randomly selected person from the local area would do (or had done) the work. Participants indicated the amount of money that they or the other person

[5] An example of a well-verified memory-based value bias is the peak-end effect. See Kahneman et al. (1993).

> should receive (or should have received) for the work, how difficult they thought the work would be (or was), and how stressed they felt when they thought about the work.
>
> Participants believed they deserved 60% more money for their future work than for their past work, but that another person deserved the same amount of money for his or her future and past work.
>
> Participants felt more stressed when they thought about their future work than when they thought about their past work, but they felt equally stressed when they thought about another person's future and past work.
>
> When feeling stressed was added to the model, it had a significant effect on the valuation of work . . . which indicates that the interactive effect of relevance and temporal location on the valuation of work was fully mediated by the stress participants felt when they imagined the work.[6]

There are two interesting features of this study for our purposes. First, it suggests that while we tend to be future-biased when it comes to our own self-interest, we aren't similarly future-biased when we consider what's in the interest of others. Second, the study proposes stress as an explanation for this self/other asymmetry. We feel stressful emotions about our own potential future suffering, emotions that "heat" our valuations. But we don't have the same emotional response when considering our own past suffering. And we don't have that emotional response when considering the options facing others.

A similar phenomenon happens with near bias. On the morning of my colonoscopy appointment, I may find myself strongly tempted to put off the procedure, even supposing it would be a bit more painful for the delay (and the additional anxiety). But if asked what I'd want for a friend—an uncomfortable procedure today or a slightly worse one several weeks from now—I don't hesitate. I think it is in my friend's interest to have the less painful one, whenever it happens.[7]

One way to test if your emotions are exerting an undue influence on your reasoning is to subject your preferences to an impartial spectator

[6] Caruso et al. (2008: 799).

[7] For discussion of philosophical issues with the self/other asymmetry in time bias see Hare (2008).

test. Imagine you were someone else, "looking in" on your situation and aware of the same information. Would you think you had formed the correct preference? Would you think your emotions are fitting? If not, then there is reason to think your preference is irrationally biased.

The impartial spectator test was developed by Adam Smith primarily as a way of explaining how we develop a moral conscience. According to Smith, we identify moral actions with actions that an impartial spectator in our society would approve of. When we wonder if our actions are moral or immoral, we imagine an impartial spectator looking in on our life. Would the impartial spectator approve of my lying to my co-workers to save face? If I think not, then I deem my lying immoral. Would the impartial spectator feel sympathy with me in preferring that my pain stop? If I think he would, then I am rational in preferring an end to the pain.

Smith explicitly applies the theory to near bias in *The Theory of Moral Sentiments*:

> In his steadily sacrificing the ease and enjoyment of the present moment for the probable expectation of the still greater ease and enjoyment of a more distant but more lasting period of time, the prudent man is always both supported and rewarded by the entire approbation of the impartial spectator, and of the representative of the impartial spectator, the man within the breast. The impartial spectator does not feel himself worn out by the present labour of those whose conduct he surveys; nor does he feel himself solicited by the importunate calls of their present appetites. To him their present, and what is likely to be their future situation, are very nearly in the same manner. He knows, however, that to the persons principally concerned, they are very different from being the same, and that they naturally affect *them* in a very different manner.[8]

According to Smith, any inclination to be near-biased disappears when we adopt the perspective of an impartial spectator. Suppose I have a colonoscopy coming up and I wish it were delayed. I definitely sympathize with my predicament—this procedure is going to be unpleasant and I'm feeling anxious about it. But I am wrong to prefer the near procedure just for its proximity, because I am overweighing my experience of fear. When I form a preference about a friend's colonoscopy, I am doing it as an impartial spectator, knowing about the relevant emotions but not experiencing them while forming the preference. In advising my

[8] See Smith (1976: Part VI). This is also discussed in Greene and Sullivan (2015: Section V).

friend not to delay her procedure, I might appeal to the same reasons featured in the Life-Saving Argument—"it'll be worse if you wait"—or the Arbitrariness Argument—"it'll still be you getting the later procedure." Smith thinks I should ignore the extra anxiety added to the predicament when I deliberate about my own preferences. I should give myself the same arguments I'd give a friend.

The impartial spectator theory has significant limitations as a complete theory of what moral and rational judgment consists in.[9] But as a more limited test of the rational fittingness of our emotions, it seems plausible. Indeed, it is operationalized in studies like the Caruso, Gilbert, and Wilson one discussed above.[10]

More cautiously, the impartial spectator test gives us some defeasible evidence of when our emotions are unduly influencing our preferences. We should be wary anytime there is a self/other asymmetry that our emotions are causing our preferences without lending justification to them. As we have seen, both near bias and future bias fail the spectator test. How should we think of these time-biased emotions if they mislead us as to what we should want?

8.3 Time Biases as Evolved Emotional Heuristics

There is a significant debate in philosophy and psychology over what exactly an emotion is and how much of what we identify as an emotion involves cognition, intentionality, or control.[11] Scottish Enlightenment philosophers like Adam Smith and David Hume thought of emotions primarily as feelings, sharply distinguished from beliefs. Other philosophers have theorized that emotions are better understood as having a cognitive dimension, and as a result, are partly susceptible to control and rational criticism. There is also a substantial debate about whether emotions are biologically hardwired or culturally mediated. Confronting these issues in any detail would take us too far afield of the main project of this

[9] For common objections, see Fleischacker (2015). For a limited defense of the project, see Raphael (2007).

[10] For a philosophical argument that we should question our temporally neutral other-regarding preferences see Hare (2008).

[11] This section draws significantly from work in Greene and Sullivan (2015: Section V).

book.[12] And it doesn't matter much for our purposes. If the cognitivists are right, then emotions are rational or irrational to the extent that they have rational or irrational preferences and beliefs as components. Recent versions of cognitivism emphasize the culturally mediated concepts that may play a role in transforming bodily sensations into full-blown manifestations of joy, anxiety, relief, and the like.[13] But let's focus here on the involuntary affective precursors of emotions. These, I hypothesize, are the likely culprits for our temporal planning errors.

On at least one prominent understanding, our dispositions towards these affective states can be viewed as adaptations whose purpose is to solve basic ecological problems facing organisms.[14] An evolutionary hypothesis suggests a theory for why we have near bias: near-biased anxiety and relief evolved as adaptations for tracking probabilities.[15] Our evolutionary ancestors had relatively short lives and faced comparatively simple planning problems. If an event is scheduled far into the future, it is "safe" to not pay much attention to it, since it will also tend to be unlikely. Best to conserve attention and decision-making for events that are scheduled sooner. In this way, evolutionary pressures selected organisms with emotions to focus on the near.[16] There is empirical work to support the view human males increase their future discount rates in response to situational factors like priming with images of attractive women, further supporting the view that the emotional component of discounting is an adaptation.[17] Now we are longer-lived organisms with more complicated plans, and we have to learn to manage these near-biased emotions. And as a matter of course we get better at managing near bias as we mature. Psychologists like Mischel who study emotional regulation identify the mechanisms by which we do this.

As with near bias, there are plausible evolutionary hypotheses about the emotions associated with future bias.[18] Just as it is advantageous to make

[12] For a survey of some of the main issues see Deigh (1994) (philosophy) and Frijda (1988) (psychology).

[13] Barrett (2017).

[14] See for instance Darwin (1896), Plutchik (1980), and Frank (1988).

[15] See Loewenstein and Elster (1992).

[16] If the social construction theory of emotion is right, these pressures could have acted on the biological precursors to emotions. Or the same kinds of pressures might have acted on the concepts that guide the construction of our emotions.

[17] Wilson and Daly (2004).

[18] Maclaurin and Dyke (2002) propose an evolutionary model for these emotions, but they do not use it to criticize the rationality of time bias; rather, it is part of their defense

tradeoffs that respect the relative probabilities of potential rewards and penalties, it is also advantageous for an organism to focus more attention and energy on what is within its control. Dwelling long enough on the past to learn from previous experiences is part of an advantageous suite of emotions. But it is more important that organisms be motivated to form preferences based on events whose probabilities they might still affect. Future events are sometimes within an organism's control but past events never are. This evolutionary explanation can be thought of as a *control heuristic* for future bias: future-directed emotions evolved to track asymmetries in control. The idea that future bias is really a form of control bias goes back at least to Hume. Like his contemporary Smith, Hume was fascinated by the complicated interplay between our emotions, beliefs, and inclinations. In the *Treatise,* he suggests an evolutionary account of future bias in our actions: "There is a phaenomenon of a like nature with the foregoing, viz *the superior effects of the same distance in futurity above that in the past.* This difference with respect to the will is easily accounted for. As none of our actions can alter the past, 'tis not strange it shou'd never determine the will."[19]

The significance of these future-directed emotions is often understood very differently from their near-biased counterparts. Weirdly, the relief and anxiety associated with future bias are often taken as evidence that future bias is rationally permissible. For example, Parfit takes the main obstacle to rejecting future bias to be that such a rejection requires us to think that one would be "irrational to be relieved when suffering is in the past" when one learns that he is the patient that has already had the surgery.[20] As we saw with the emotion defense in the last chapter, this is similar to the cases involving near bias. We might think that our emotional response is "hard-wired" and must be dealt with in other aspects of our rational planning. We have no reason to treat future-biased emotions any differently than near-biased ones in our account of prudential rationality.

The evolutionary account of time biases gives us a theory of error for why we've been tempted to discount both the past and distant future, even

of the B-theory against Prior's "Thank Goodness That's Over" argument. The evolutionary model is also suggested by Horwich (1992: 196–8) and Suhler and Callender (2012).

[19] Hume (2000: Section 2.3.7.6).

[20] See Parfit (1984: 186). Parfit ultimately remains neutral regarding the rationality of future bias.

if it isn't prudentially rational to have such attitudes. You have a bias (in our terminology) if you are systematically disposed to form a preference that is not adequately based in reasons.[21] Many well-known biases have evolutionary explanations and time biases are no different.[22] Our time-biased emotions are adaptive, which offers an explanation for why we have them. And for the kinds of scenarios our evolutionary ancestors needed to reason about, they were highly successful. Indeed, for times when we are not capable of sustained deliberation about our reasons, it isn't such a bad idea to rely on the direction these emotions provide. They play a crucial role in what psychologists call our System 1 cognition, our automatic reasoning about predicaments. But when it comes to System 2 cognition—the kind most relevant to forming and executing plans—we want our preferences to be adequately based in reasons. And as we saw in the foregoing chapters, there are plenty of good reasons to be temporally neutral.

Note further that evolutionary heuristic theories like this can be generalized beyond just emotion-based explanations. Not all heuristic biases have an emotional component; for example, it is unclear there is an emotional component to our biases in judging probabilities. It is just that, as a matter of course, the most significant rational struggle with overcoming time biases comes in processing the ways such emotions distort our ability to correctly value events. And the emotional dimension plays a central role in explaining the self/other asymmetries in discounting.[23]

8.4 Two Mistakes about Temporal Neutrality

With this theory of error in mind, we might wonder how we should change. What would it mean to become a temporally neutral planner?

[21] Being indifferent is treated as a kind of preference here, so indifference can also be biased—as in the Lucretian death asymmetry in Chapter 7.

[22] For instance, Kahneman gives an evolutionary explanation of loss aversion. "Organisms that treat threats as more urgent than opportunities have a better chance to survive and reproduce" (Kahneman 2011: 282).

[23] The evolved emotional heuristic theory also explains why we are prone to discount some goods (like pains and pleasures) but are more neutral with respect to other goods like achievements. Different, more socially mediated emotions like pride and shame accompany goods like achievements and failures, and given that these goods already require substantial planning and now-for-later tradeoffs, there was less need for their attendant emotions to be temporally asymmetric. The theory of temporal neutrality again generates a hypothesis about emotion and judgment that could be measured by psychologists.

To the extent that the issue has been considered, temporal neutrality is often characterized as a form either of cold-hearted stoicism or of alienating optimism. Both portrayals are misleading.

On the stoic interpretation, the temporally neutral agent trains herself so when she realizes her death is approaching, she feels no fear, since she has valuable life still in her past. The temporally neutral agent suppresses her excitement at the prospect of a great new adventure, since she sees no difference between projects she has already completed and projects she has yet to begin.

This is absurd. Temporal neutrality—at least the kind advocated here—doesn't assume anything about our ability to control our emotions or the desirability of muting them. Indeed, there are many instances when our emotional reactions contribute positively to our plans. The fact that we experience joy and excitement before starting a new project means that project contributes more to our well-being over the course of our lives than if we approached it with cold indifference. While it is irrational to fear death but not prefer to have already lived longer, the emotions that inevitably accompany contemplating mortality can make our current experiences more poignant and can, appropriately processed, add value to our lives. Temporal neutrality requires us to plan around our emotions and to prefer emotions that enhance well-being over emotions that diminish it. It does not require blindly suppressing our time-biased emotions.

Others have interpreted temporal neutrality as a strategy for ignoring suffering and directing our attention and emotional reserves towards good moments in time. In *Slaughterhouse Five*, Kurt Vonnegut imagines a race of temporally neutral aliens, the Trafalmadoreans, who can perceive every moment of time directly. They choose not to dwell on any instant that disturbs them, and this attitude becomes a model for the Earthling protagonist, Billy Pilgrim, in dealing with his traumatic experiences in World War II. Describing the Trafalmadoreans, Vonnegut writes:

> They can see how permanent all the moments are, and they can look at any moment that interests them. It is just an illusion we have here on Earth that one moment follows from another one, like beads on a string, and that once a moment is gone it is gone forever. When a Trafalmadorean sees a corpse, all he thinks is that the dead person is in bad condition in that particular moment, but the same person is just fine in plenty of other moments. Now when I [Billy] hear that

somebody is dead, I simply shrug and say what the Trafalmadoreans say about dead people, which is 'So it goes.'[24]

But temporal neutrality does not entail Trafalmadorean optimism. For one, temporal neutrality does not presuppose that time does not pass. The arguments of this book are perfectly consistent with A-theories of time, which presuppose objective differences between the past, present, and future and deny that time is spread out the same way space is. On the usual A-theory metaphysic, you are not the "same person" after your death—you don't exist, you are no longer part of the concrete objective reality. If an A-theory is right, the Trafalmadorean preferences are based on fantasy and not good reasons.

More importantly, as beings located in space and time, we inevitably experience events in a set order. Try as we might, we cannot "unstick" ourselves from time the way that Billy and Trafalmadoreans do. So we are saddled with our actual, adaptive, temporally asymmetric emotions. Again, we can plan around them. But there is little reason to think we can or should eliminate any of them.

8.5 Planning in Neutral

If you are temporally neutral, you are indifferent between whether good or bad events happen in your past, present, and future. Given the choice between a more painful past surgery and a less painful future one, you prefer the future one, holding fixed facts about the temporally asymmetric emotions preceding and following the event. You prefer more of a good life to less, but you are indifferent as to whether your best years are behind you or still yet to come. When you can control your emotions, you do so in a way that will help you have the best life possible. This is temporal neutrality in its broadest strokes.

In the preceding chapters, we have also seen some more specific strategies you should follow in order to be more temporally neutral in your planning. It is worth tying them together now.

First, you should not allow temporal features like how far in the future an event is scheduled to cloud your judgments about risk. To test whether

[24] Vonnegut (1969: 27).

your preferences are near-biased rather than risk-tolerant, you might try a reverse lottery thought experiment. Figure out how likely an event is to happen—for instance getting diabetes from your lifestyle or converting your savings into a retirement windfall. Imagine entering a lottery for that event tomorrow with the same odds and holding fixed (as much as possible) the subsequent effects on your life and duration of your plans. If your preferences about the event stay roughly the same, that is evidence your preferences are based on appropriate probabilistic reasons. But if they change, that's a flag you are being near-biased.

Second, as we've seen in this chapter, you can likewise test for undue influence of your emotions by asking what the impartial spectator would make of your preferences. The impartial spectator test gives us a method for disentangling the emotions that are causing our preferences from the emotions that provide reasons to back our preferences. As with the reverse lottery, this test has limits. For instance, the test will not be helpful in cases where our preferences are responding to purely egocentric reasons (if there are such reasons). And there may be cases where our bias has no attendant emotional mechanism, and so it manifests both when we reason for ourselves and when we reason for others we care about. Still, the test is useful in many cases where we confuse our emotions with our reasons.

Third, according to temporal neutrality, events have accurate, permanent values for you. As Plato counsels, you should try to figure out what those values are, especially when you face tradeoffs involving those events. Otherwise, you are liable to make incorrect sacrifices, as we saw in the Life-Saving, Mixed Tradeoff, and No Regrets Arguments. We are most likely to make mistakes about these values when we are trading in pains and pleasures, so be extra deliberative when planning around those. If asked to set a fair value on how much you should be compensated for an onerous job you've already done, don't just guess at a value. First, try to vividly remember what it was like to suffer the past experience. Likewise, if asked whether you'd like to invest in a somewhat distant opportunity, try to vividly imagine what it will be like to receive the good before you decide how much you'll trade for it.[25]

[25] There is an interesting question of when you are best situated to perceive the accurate value of an experience (i.e., while you are experiencing it? afterward? prospectively?). I hope to take up this question for temporal neutrality in future work.

Fourth, you aren't just a momentary stage making a one-off decision and then marching out of the theater. You are allowed to think of your plans perspectivally and from the present vantage point. You also can and should think of yourself as someone with a past and a future. Indeed, you should be careful of absent-mindedly endorsing the "multiple-self" talk that philosophers favor. You need not always think of yourself as a short stage making a sacrifice for some other stage—at least absent some great metaphysical argument for that view. Planning in terms of detached stages might make it harder for you to be motivated by your egoistic reasons. And as we saw in Chapter 4, you should be wary of ways your egoistic concern might be biased, especially when you are planning around changes that affect your moral capacities or social standing.

Fifth, as a temporally neutral agent you are permitted to take your anticipated future preferences into account when deciding what to do. You need not succumb to temptation and you need not "screw" yourself at future times by committing to plans you will regret. Which raises a question: can you take your remembered *past* preferences into account as well? More on that in the next chapter.

9

Neutrality, Sunk Costs, and Commitment

> Never give in, never give in, never, never, never, never—in nothing, great or small, large or petty—never give in except to convictions of honor and good sense.
>
> Winston Churchill, *Address to Harrow School*

In the next three chapters, we will consider some of the surprising ways that temporally neutral agents reason differently than their time-biased counterparts. For instance, temporally neutral agents sometimes take their *past* preferences into account when deciding whether to complete projects. On one way of looking at it, to defer to your past preferences is to engage in a cardinal sin of rational planning: honoring sunk costs. As *Economics for Dummies* puts it, "Rationally speaking, you should consider only the *future*, potential marginal costs and benefits of your *future* options."[1] Only a complete dummy takes her past preferences and choices as reasons to stick to a plan she no longer prefers.

But on another way of looking at it, agents who consider their past commitments are demonstrating a kind of integrity—one that can be a great virtue when it comes to making and sticking with complicated plans. And given the arguments of previous chapters, why should we think it *obvious* that rational agents only focus on the future?

Temporal neutrality and the phenomenon of sunk cost reasoning will be the focus of this chapter. I'll show you how to use the theory of temporal neutrality developed in earlier chapters to distinguish rationally permissible deference to past plans from irrational sunk cost reasoning. And I'll compare the temporally neutral approach with other theories

[1] Flynn (2011: 33). Emphasis is mine.

philosophers have offered to explain why we sometimes take our past preferences as reason-giving.

9.1 The Sunk Cost Puzzle

To get us started, it will help to have some examples of deference to the past. Examples like these supply some of the data a theory of rational planning needs to accommodate. Here is one:

> **Triathlon:** Suppose a few months ago you registered for a triathlon. Over the intervening months, you have logged many hours of training and swore not to merely watch the race from the sidelines. You always preferred to compete. Today is race day. The weather is fine, you are healthy, and you haven't gained any new information about the race. But you just aren't "feeling it"—you now prefer not to compete. Suppose further that you predict tomorrow (and going forward) you'll be indifferent about whether you competed. You don't anticipate any regrets. Is it rationally permissible to compete, even though now you prefer not to and tomorrow you won't care?

Considering this case, I think most of us think it is permissible to compete. Rationality wouldn't require you to compete, but the fact that competing would complete a longstanding plan of yours licenses you to ignore your cold feet.

Consider another thought experiment:

> **Dragon Sagas:** George has spent most of his career working on a series of seven pulp fantasy books called *The Dragon Sagas*. He is nearly finished with the final volume. Another few days of work would complete the project. Ever since he conceived of the series early in his career, he has wanted to finish it: he did not want to die without explaining the fate of his fictional kingdom. He learns he only has a few days to live and finds himself, now, just barely preferring not to finish. And because he has such a short time left, he doesn't predict that finishing the final book will matter either way for his life going forward. He wonders if it is rational to spend any time now trying to tie up his last "loose end." Is it rationally permissible for George to finish the book?

Presumably it is rationally permissible for George to spend his remaining days finishing the book, even if it won't contribute to his life going forward (since he has no life going forward). His past plans give him a reason to prefer finishing now.

Consider one more thought experiment:

> **Rice Cooker:** A few months ago, Peter purchased a rice cooker. At the time he preferred to cook more rice—he figured if he started a habit of using it, he would save money on weeknight dinners. But in fact he has rarely used it and he doubts he will develop the habit. Tonight Peter leans towards ordering pizza rather than cooking rice. As he's picking up the phone, he sees the cooker on his counter. He reasons that because he once had that plan and made the investment in the appliance, he has some reason to use it. Is it rationally permissible for Peter to opt for a rice dinner on that basis?

I take it most of us can sympathize with Peter. I'm certainly guilty of making appliance investments that don't quite pay off. But in this case, we are less confident that Peter is reasoning well when he takes his past investment and plan as reasons to currently prefer cooking rice. In economic terms, the rice cooker investment is a sunk cost—a past investment that Peter can do nothing to change now. And as a matter of course, Peter has not developed any habit of rice cooking and does not anticipate developing such a habit. If he has changed his mind about the rice plan, he should go ahead and order a pizza.

A theory of rational planning should explain why sticking to constant plans to run triathlons or finish fantasy heptalogies can be rationally permissible, but honoring wishy-washy plans to use your rice cooker is irrational. More generally, a theory of rational planning owes us an answer to *the sunk cost puzzle*: is there any principled way to distinguish irrational instances of honoring of sunk costs from acceptable fulfillment of past intentions? Surely part of the answer has to do with the pattern of commitment the agents have demonstrated towards their plan, not just their present and future preferences about the plan. Or so I will argue here. Generalizing the theory of temporal neutrality from Chapters 1–8 can help us develop a plausible answer to the sunk cost puzzle.

9.2 Weak Forecasting and Weak Honoring

In Chapter 6, we considered when it is permissible to take your anticipated future preferences into account in making a decision. I argued that predictions about your future preferences can play a role, particularly in cases where you realize you are being momentarily tempted by one of your options. The principle we needed for the arguments was a very weak rational reflection principle:

> **Weak Forecasting:** If you have and always will have all of the relevant information about the options available to you, then it is permissible for you to prefer any option you know you will never regret in favor of one you know you will eventually regret.

Remember that in this context "regret" just means to prefer to have chosen otherwise. With principles like this, we allow that your preferences might change over time. The big idea behind forecasting is that if your preferences are going to solidify around one of your options in the future, it is permissible to prefer it (and choose it) right now, even if it violates your present preferences.

Temporally neutral agents do not think the fact that some event occurred in the past or distant future is any reason (by itself) to care more or less about it. Which raises a question—Weak Forecasting says we can take into account our future preferences when making decisions. Is it also permissible to prefer and act only to satisfy your *past* preferences? I think it is, at least on some occasions, because I think temporal neutrality also recommends a past-directed rational reflection principle.

You *foreswear* some option when you prefer that you not choose it in the future. Foreswearing is the mirror image of regret and is likewise part of a rational strategy for pursuing long-term plans, especially when you can anticipate future temptations. For instance, I might foreswear having a second drink at dinner, preferring that I not choose it when the waiter returns to the table. With this notion of foreswearing, we can state the past-directed version of Weak Forecasting. Let's define a plan at a time as a choice for one set of future options over another. For instance you might form a plan to run a triathlon (and train accordingly). Or you might form a plan to become a rice eater. Let t_1 be a past time when a plan was chosen.

> **Weak Honoring:** If from t_1 you have, always have had, and always will have all of the relevant information about the options available to you, then it is permissible to choose any option you have never foresworn and will never regret over any option you have foresworn or will regret.

Weak Honoring follows from Weak Forecasting and our theory that any differences between past and future events (like the event of forming a preference) are arbitrary. It also explains why it is rationally permissible to run the race and finish the book series. In both of these scenarios, there is an option that has never been foresworn and will never be regretted. But Weak Honoring doesn't similarly justify Peter's rice cooker logic, since presumably Peter prefers now (and going forward) that he had never invested in the appliance, and there are many past times when he has foresworn his plan to use it.

Of course, like Weak Forecasting, this principle is highly idealized. We very rarely face choices where our preferences about the options within a plan are totally unwavering. In Chapter 6, we also described a more sophisticated variant of the Forecasting strategy—Balanced Forecasting—that permits you to choose paths of occasional regret over paths of frequent regret. We can likewise develop a balanced version of honoring that permits you to balance the constancy of your past commitments with your anticipated future regrets. But it will be easier to present the arguments for temporal neutrality with the idealized Weak Forecasting and Weak Honoring, so we will stick with those versions for now.

According to the theory of temporal neutrality, what's distinctive about irrational sunk cost reasoning (compared with more benign forms of honoring past preferences) is that sunk cost reasoning honors a past preference even when the agent now regrets ever having that preference (or anticipates regretting it in the future). Your past preferences should now be disregarded if you think they were based on bad information or if, going forward, you prefer an option that is incompatible with your past plans. But past preferences can license current preferences and actions in the absence of foreseen regret. Moreover, as with other time biases, sometimes the activation of our emotions can distort our preferences. The fact that an agent is now experiencing the guilt associated with reneging on a past commitment does not supply any new reason to honor a plan. One hallmark of traditionally bad sunk cost reasoning is that the agent takes the present experience of such an emotion as offering new present reasons.

9.3 Sunk Costs and "Rational Irrationality"?

To better understand the temporally neutral approach to rational commitment, it will be helpful to contrast this theory with other analyses of sunk cost reasoning. One prominent response to the sunk cost puzzle distinguishes ideal from non-ideal strategies. Suppose I know that I am highly susceptible to temptation. I form long-term plans, only to abandon them in moments of weakness. It might be adaptive for someone like me to take facts about my past investments as reasons to stick to a plan, since otherwise I would never get the benefits that come from long-term plans. There is some evidence that sunk cost reasoning helps motivate individuals to stick with their plans. For example, consider this recent *New York Times* story on the demands of training for elite Ironman triathlons:

> James O'Connor, 44, who lives in Far Hills, N.J., and works in asset management, said that after the wear and tear of decades of commuting and working, he had committed to doing his second Ironman triathlon in November 2016.
>
> For him, there are certainly financial costs. It cost $700 to enter the Ironman in Tempe, Ariz., and travel costs will be much more. He plans to do two half-Ironman triathlons for training. And then there is the gear needed to train and compete in events that encompass swimming, biking and running. He estimated that cost at more than $1,000.
>
> But those expenses are not Mr. O'Connor's primary concern. What motivates him are the larger costs, in economic terms, of what he will miss this year. He got his work colleagues and his family to sign off on his participation since they will see him less. He also enlisted a friend to train with him and committed to raising money for charity so he will not be doing the Ironman solely for himself.
>
> "The Ironman is a very selfish race," he said. "It's a huge amount of personal commitment. The more people who are part of it, the less selfish it seems."
>
> Keeping in mind what he is sacrificing to accomplish his resolution will, he said, keep him on track.[2]

For some would-be athletes like O'Connor, focusing on what he has already sacrificed helps motivate him to act on his plans, even when his sources of present motivation falter. If he feels like taking a day off training, the shame of letting down his friends and family might motivate him to act against his present preferences. On race day, if he is tempted to abandon the plan there is nothing he can do to recoup his money or lost family time, so these should not feature as any reasons for his preferences. But in the long run, it is good that he feels the tug of the sunk cost argument, since it helps him overcome his temptation to flake and thereby indirectly helps him realize his longer-term goal of completing an Ironman.

[2] Sullivan (2016).

Robert Nozick justifies sunk cost reasoning as a non-ideal strategy:

> We can knowingly employ our tendency to take sunk costs seriously as a means of increasing our *future* rewards. If this tendency is irrational, it can be rationally utilized to check and overcome another irrationality. If someone offered us a pill that henceforth would make us people who never honored sunk costs, we might be ill advised to accept it; it would deprive us of a valuable tool for getting past temptations of the (future) moment.[3]

In other words, even if strictly speaking it is not rational to defer to your past preferences, given that we are non-ideal planners, honoring sunk costs might be part of our best strategy for overcoming temptation and realizing long-term investments. If you took a pill to forget all of your past preferences and commitments, you would be far more susceptible to temptation. In this sense, such reasoning is "rational irrationality"—rational insofar as it contributes to success, even if, by Nozick's lights, our past preferences do not bear any rational weight. Likewise, we might think we have adapted an aversion to wastefulness, because worrying about waste makes us likely to be more efficient husbands of resources going forward and not because we have any reason to not waste our past investments. Finally, a tendency to honor sunk costs might be a good game-theoretic strategy for agents, since it signals a tendency to fulfill commitments in joint projects.[4]

This strategy treats sunk cost reasoning as a useful heuristic. Just as we may plausibly have developed time-biased anxiety to help us quickly gauge probabilities and to mirror potential for control, we might have also developed emotions of shame around wastefulness in order to better stick to our projects. But as we saw in Chapter 8, it is not always rational to defer to a generally useful heuristic. When you have enough time and attention to properly deliberate about your reasons, you shouldn't rely on the heuristic. You should deliberate directly on your reasons. Indeed, while finishing triathlons might be easier for a certain stubborn sort of character, this same trait disposes an agent to continue to waste counter space on undesired appliances. Or (in the more serious economic cases) to continue to sink funds into projects that they persistently regret undertaking. Finally, this indirect defense of sunk cost reasoning cannot

[3] Nozick (1993: 23).
[4] See Kelly (2004) for discussion of some of these indirect arguments.

explain why it is rationally permissible to fulfill past plans in the Triathlon and Dragon Saga cases. The agents do not have to make snap decisions. By hypothesis, they are not overcome with emotion or unable to appreciate their reasons. They have accounted for all of the future ramifications of their decisions. And in the case of Dragon Sagas, George has no reason to signal his commitment to others, since he won't need to cooperate with anyone ever again. So the non-ideal theory answer to the sunk cost puzzle misses some of the data and fails to differentiate the intuitively permissible and impermissible cases of honoring.

9.4 Sunk Costs and Rational Non-Reconsideration?

A different but related approach to the sunk cost puzzle emphasizes the important role that intentions play in our planning. Future-directed intentions are controlling—they should lead you to make a certain decision at a future time. And they are stable—once you've formed an intention, the future decision is relatively immune from reconsideration or revision.[5] As Richard Holton puts it, in forming an intention you raise the threshold for the relevance of new information towards judging the rational status of your plan.[6] If I am deciding at t_1 whether to compete in a triathlon, there might be many details that I entertain as relevant—who else will compete, what shoes could I wear, what temperature will the water be? But once I've formed the intention to compete, I close off consideration of many of these smaller details. Discovering I was slightly incorrect in my prediction of the water temperature shouldn't move me to reconsider competing, while discovering there are sharks in the water might meet the new threshold for relevance. Forming intentions (and following through on them) is important for imperfect planners like us, who must efficiently process information and execute plans that require sequences of dependent decisions.

What appears to be sunk cost reasoning could be understood instead as cases of rational non-reconsideration of intentions.[7] In the Triathlon and Dragon Sagas cases from Section 9.1, an intention was formed—compete

[5] Bratman (1987) and Holton (2009). [6] Holton (2009: 2).
[7] See Chapter 7 of Holton (2009).

in the race, finish the book series. The threshold for reconsidering or revising the decision was thereby raised. The fact that the agent barely prefers not following through does not meet the threshold for being relevant. It is rational to form and act on intentions (and to have the corresponding habit of not reconsidering them or revising them lightly). So it is rationally permissible to compete or finish the books in these cases. Indeed, rational commitment pressures the agent to ignore the new information about her preferences. In this sense, the intention-based account of sunk cost reasoning does more than license honoring past preferences—it can require us to honor them.

Note also that this strategy could equally support Peter's rice cooker reasoning. He formed the intention to develop the rice-cooking habit, raising the threshold for relevant new information. The fact that he now somewhat prefers pizza to rice might likewise fail to meet the new threshold for relevance. Indeed, he might lean towards pizza every moment after buying the rice cooker, but never enough to clear the revised threshold for relevance. So the intention-based response to the sunk cost puzzle threatens to license the controversial cases of honoring sunk costs in the process of explaining the innocent ones. More generally, this theory of intentions has the odd result that even if you now regret your previous intention, and even if that regret is properly based in reasons, and even if you predict you'll *always* continue to regret the past intention, as long as the regret is not based on sufficiently weighty new reasons, your past intention rationally licenses honoring your sunk cost. But cases like these are the paradigm of irrational honoring.

Note also that this approach to the sunk cost puzzle is a non-ideal theory, like Nozick's solution surveyed above. If we had time enough to always deliberate about our reasons, we would not need to develop habits of rational non-reconsideration. So, like Nozick's solution, it won't explain why there seem to be cases where fully apprised, well-reasoning, unpressured agents honor sunk costs. And it won't explain why an agent like George at the end of his life has any reason to continue to cultivate the habit of non-reconsideration.

As I see it, Weak Honoring has three advantages over the non-ideal theories of honoring past commitments. First, Weak Honoring can explain why even unpressured agents who are fully apprised of their reasons might rationally prefer to complete a merely past plan. Second, Weak Honoring can explain why it is rationally permissible to honor past plans even when there is no future for the agent. Third, Weak Honoring is part of a systematic theory of rational planning (the theory of temporal neutrality) while these strategies are more ad hoc, describing exceptions to a typically future-biased approach to rational planning.

9.5 Temporal Neutrality and Rational Commitment

Given a defensible assumption about rational commitment, we can also offer another, more direct motivation for Weak Honoring. Recall the Triathlon case. Suppose it is the day to register for the race, and you know ahead of time how your preferences are likely to shift over time. That is, you know that during training you will always prefer to compete. And you know on race day you will prefer not to compete. And you know afterward you will be indifferent. You also know you will not gain or lose any reasons or rational capacity during this time. And you are a preference permissivist about triathlons: you do not think your reasons rationally require one of the options over the other at any given time. Would it be rationally permissible to commit to compete now, even knowing you'll briefly have cold feet on race day and indifference later?

I'm inclined to think committing to the race is rationally permissible in these circumstances. But this would be difficult to explain if only present and future preferences can be relevant to rational planning. Here is one plausible auxiliary assumption about rational commitment:

> **Permissible Follow Through:** Rational commitment to a plan at t_1 requires predicting it will be rationally permissible to prefer to follow through with the plan if you do not gain new reasons not to.

In other words, you cannot rationally commit to a plan that you predict would require you to be irrational when completing it. Permissible Follow Through and the view that only present or future preferences are relevant to rational planning would, together, entail it is rationally impermissible to sign up for the triathlon. But this is too restrictive, so either Permissible Follow Through is false or facts about your past preferences could make it rationally permissible for you to compete on race day. Which is it?

Permissible Follow Through is admittedly a strong criterion for rational planning. For instance, it delivers a decisive verdict in a version of Kavka's famous toxin puzzle.[8] Suppose Dr. Evil is an adept detector of rational commitment. He offers you the following bargain. If you rationally commit now to drink a toxin tomorrow, then tonight he will pay you a million dollars. The toxin will make you temporarily very ill, but will otherwise have no lasting consequences. Further, once the money is in your account, you are perfectly free to change your mind about drinking the toxin. You can predict now, with certainty, that you will rationally prefer not to drink the toxin tomorrow morning. By then either you'll have a million dollars in your account or not, but either way your life will not go better for drinking the toxin. So according to Permissible Follow Through, you could not rationally commit now to a plan to drink the toxin, even if you think such a plan would benefit you to the tune of a million dollars. This might seem like a controversial result, though the toxin puzzle is an enduring puzzle precisely because none of the available options seem obviously rationally permissible. As I mentioned in the Introduction, I think we should be open to the possibility of rational dilemmas, and Permissible Follow Through combined with the Success principle might create one such dilemma, at least in toxin cases.

In more ordinary cases of rational planning, Permissible Follow Through seems well-motivated. Whenever I engage in an investment that requires now-for-later tradeoffs, the rationality of my plan depends on me predicting (at least) that I will later follow through and gain the deferred benefit. It is rationally self-defeating to invest in a plan whose success requires me later being irrational in its execution. This does not preclude changing my mind about the plan halfway through. It only requires that whatever my preferences end up being, it could remain rationally permissible for me to stick with the plan. This constraint on rational commitment gives further motivation for temporal neutrality.

9.6 Sunk Costs and Structuralism?

Some other proposed solutions to the sunk cost puzzle do not treat honoring as a heuristic or non-ideal strategy, but rather try to explain how some kinds of merely past preferences could be presently reason-giving. One such strategy appeals to structuralism about the value of a

[8] Kavka (1983).

life. Recall from Chapter 2, structuralists hold that the value of a whole life might depend on the order of goods within the life. And the value that a particular event contributes to your life might depend on what happens after that event. For example, in the Triathlon case, you might decide to run the race in order to redeem all of your past training efforts—a life where you strived for a goal and then achieved that goal is significantly better than one where you strived in vain. Tom Kelly hypothesizes that what separates permissible honoring of past projects from impermissible sunk cost reasoning is that in the former case, you have some independent reason now for preferring a project (i.e., there is at least some independent reason to value finishing a triathlon), and the fact that you'd also redeem some past efforts gives you decisive reason now to finish the project.[9]

This structuralist theory seems to make sense of the permissible cases of sticking to projects (i.e., triathlons and dragon sagas). But it doesn't explain why Peter would be irrational in taking his rice cooker investment as a reason to eat rice now. Suppose Peter gave himself the following argument for honoring his sunk investment: "I have some independent reason now to eat rice—it is healthy and economical. That reason is not decisive right now, but if I cook the rice, I will redeem my past purchase. I will make my life one where I successfully planned and finished a rice cooking project, rather than one where I abandoned the project." The argument seems foolish—a life where one successfully cooks rice is *not* structurally better than a life where one orders pizza.

We might try to strengthen the structuralist solution by adding an additional qualification—honoring sunk costs is rationally permissible when (i) there is independent reason now to stick with the project, (ii) sticking with the project would redeem past efforts, *and* (iii) the project is a genuine achievement. Since cooking rice is no great achievement, Peter's reasoning would fail this test. But perhaps finishing dragon sagas and triathlons does pass the test for being achievements. Thomas Hurka justifies some instances of sunk cost reasoning on precisely these lines: "People frequently act intending in part to help achieve some goal in the future. Whether this intention adds to their perfection now depends, given a success view, on whether the goal is achieved, which again is settled later.

[9] Kelly (2004: 76).

Given these facts, success versions of perfectionism can require people to promote goods in the past."[10] Recall from Chapter 5, Hurka thinks that we do not discount events that we value for perfectionist reasons (like discoveries). So perhaps it makes sense that the passage of time never affects an agent's preferences about achievements.

Where Kelly's structuralist solution to the sunk cost puzzle is too permissive, Hurka's structuralist solution is too restrictive. For one, there are cases where it is permissible to defer to your past preferences even though the project you are engaged in is not a human perfection in any reasonable sense of the term. For example:

> **Castles in the Sand:** Amelia has spent the past few hours working on an elaborate sand castle with the intent of smashing it. For every moment since she has started the project, she has preferred smashing it to abandoning the castle intact. Now the castle is nearly done and she finds she is leaning towards leaving it. She knows she won't care either way going forward. Amelia reasons to herself: "I built this castle with the intent of smashing it. I may as well go ahead and smash it."

Amelia's preference to smash the castle is rationally permissible. But there is no way that building and destroying sand castles counts as a perfection in a life. Any good biography of Amelia would be justified in omitting the castle episode. Hurka's version of structuralism cannot explain trivial but permissible cases of honoring. Weak Honoring can—this case has exactly the same structure of regret and foreswearing as the original Triathlon case.

The perfectionist defense of honoring sunk costs is also vulnerable to an arbitrariness objection, since the theory draws a sharp distinction between the value of attempting but failing to fully complete some goal and the value of attempting and succeeding. According to the theory, it is rational to sometimes honor sunk costs because for perfectionist projects the benefit of fully succeeding is significantly different (and more valuable) to a life than the benefit of getting close and not quite succeeding. But the difference between success and failure for many perfectionist projects can come down to small and arbitrary details. Consider one way of pursuing the perfection of achieving an education:

[10] Hurka (1996: 110–11).

Oxford Graduation: Obtaining a degree from Oxford University is a drawn-out process. First you matriculate. Then you spend years studying. Then you sit for a variety of different exams. If you are successful in your exams, you will get "leave to supplicate" from your program and college, which is essentially permission to graduate. Graduation ceremonies are scheduled months or years after leave is granted. A graduation requires some onerous paperwork and fees, as well as a brief crash course in bowing and Latin oath-taking. Some students schedule graduation and officially earn their degree. Some never schedule it, instead reporting the date of successful completion of their exams on their vitae. Suppose Mary and Steph are two philosophy masters degree students at Oxford. Both received leave to supplicate. Mary always preferred to graduate; Steph was one of the students who never particularly cared. Only Mary followed through and graduated. Both ended up with good philosophy jobs.

Graduation is the final step in completing an Oxford education. Is Steph's life any worse than Mary's for lacking the accomplishment of graduating from her program? Presumably not—it came down to just some paperwork, scheduling, and fees! Actually finishing this project has no tangible impact on one's future prospects. Would prudence recommend doing the paperwork, paying the fee, and going through with the ceremony even if she never preferred to graduate? Also presumably not. Both Mary and Steph's preferences about finishing are perfectly rationally permissible. Indeed, many of the goods appealed to in perfectionist accounts of well-being can contribute value at every stage of the plan, not just at the very end.

Finally, the perfectionist defense of commitment requires thinking that achievements are in principle more valuable than failures. But, we might think there are many cases where a failed project contributes more structuralist value to a person's life. In 1944, Claus von Stauffenberg attempted to lead a coup d'état against Hitler. His project failed, and led to his execution by the Nazis. But the way his project failed made his life a story of heroic and selfless martyrdom, contributing a kind of value that arguably outweighs the value of a life where von Stauffenberg succeeds and becomes a temporary leader of reconstructed Germany.[11]

[11] This case comes from Adams (2010).

The structuralist answers to the sunk cost puzzle tend to be either too permissive (i.e., permit redemptive rice cooker purchases) or too demanding (i.e., require a success-based perfectionist theory of value). Moreover, any of the structuralist theories will inherit the more general puzzles for structuralism we surveyed in Chapter 2. For these reasons, we shouldn't look to structuralism to solve the sunk cost puzzle.

9.7 Sunk Costs and Integrity?

We often criticize people who make commitments and then fail to follow through as lacking in integrity. Moral integrity is the disposition to stick to your moral commitments in the face of temptation. Prudential integrity is the disposition to stick to your self-interested plans in the face of temptation. Could the value of prudential integrity help answer the sunk cost puzzle?

Suppose Alan registers for a triathlon, trains for months, buys the race T-shirt, new running shoes, and high-calorie gels. But then on the day of the race he decides that he prefers not to run it. Some onlookers might criticize Alan for wasting his time and money preparing for the race. Others might criticize Alan for not "redeeming" his lost investment. But still others might criticize Alan for lacking a certain integrity in his planning. Indeed, we can value prudential integrity even when there isn't a significant moral dimension to one's choices. The non-technical term for people like Alan is "flake." Flakes are unreliable—they form plans, even seemingly insignificant ones, but then often fail to follow through. Flaky choices can be a moral failing, especially in circumstances where others are depending upon you to fulfill your commitments. But many cases of flakiness—like Alan's—don't raise any moral flags. And we don't criticize Alan merely because he missed the opportunity of completing a triathlon—many of us never run such races and certainly don't deserve criticism. We judge characters like Alan because their preferences are incoherent. Observing this pattern, we think less of him as a planner. And making and following through with plans is an important part of what makes us persons in the first place. As Cicero exhorted us back in the epigraph to Chapter 4, what's distinctive of man is our ability to join together the stages of our lives through plans. Imagine that January rolls around again and Alan once again declares his intention to run a triathlon. Not only would we think him foolhardy for investing in the project again, we'd also, I think, be less likely to take his plan seriously *as a plan*, since plans require a certain degree of coherence of preferences.

Christine Korsgaard thinks that our ability to plan and act just is our ability to pull ourselves together into integrated agents over time. Because she thinks action requires integrity, she thinks that the "multiple self" models of future planning we surveyed in Chapter 4 are inaccurate:

> To ask why the present self should cooperate with the future ones is to assume that the present self has reasons with which it already identifies, and which are independent of those of later selves. Perhaps it is natural to think of the present self as necessarily concerned with present satisfaction. But it is mistaken. In order to make deliberative choices, your present self must identify with something from which you will derive your reasons, but not necessarily with something present. The sort of thing you identify yourself with may carry you automatically into the future . . . Indeed, the choice of any action, no matter how trivial, takes you some way into the future . . . And to the extent that you regulate your choices by identifying yourself as the one who is implementing something like a particular plan of life, you need to identify with your future in order to be *what you are even now*. When the person is viewed as an agent, no clear content can be given to the idea of a *merely* present self.[12]

This concept of integrity has interesting applications for our current topic. Korsgaard thinks an important source of reasons for our actions comes from our practical identities, which stretch out over time. Reflect on any sufficiently short moment of your life (maybe the past few minutes) and ask what your preferences in that interval were. Some were probably limited to that interval—you might have preferred to have a snack or a warmer cup of coffee rather than no snack and cold coffee. You might have wished that this chapter be a bit shorter. But that is just a small and non-representative sample of your preferences in that interval. If you are a normal, planning human agent, you probably have preferences that look out into the future. You prefer that you finish this book (rather than not). You are planning for your career, and you hope that this is a good use of your time. You prefer that your children get into a good college rather than be frustrated in their ambitions. You hope we sort out a long-term solution to climate change before it is too late. Being a person means having such plans and hopes, often rooted in our different social identities. You will finish this book because you are a philosopher.

[12] Korsgaard (1989: 113–14). Emphasis is mine. Korsgaard further develops this theory in Korsgaard (2009).

You will save for your child because you are a parent. And being a person means actively conforming your choices to these plans and hopes, rather than merely passively experiencing bouts of pleasure or pain. So, contrary to what might be suggested by the multiple selves model, the present self (whatever that is) is a *self* primarily because it has these forward-reaching plans and hopes.

Just as our practical identities carry us into the future, they can also carry us into the past. Nobody wakes up one morning a triathlete, a parent, or a philosopher. These practical identities are the product of choices we've made and commitments we've incurred in the past. You couldn't construct a practical identity if you constantly changed your plans or reneged on your previous commitments.

This suggests a different defense of honoring, based on the necessity of having a practical identity. In brief: to engage in rational planning at all, you need a unified practical identity. You need to be able to think of yourself not just as a bundle of preferences, but as philosopher, parent, athlete, etc. Constructing such an identity requires sticking with your plans over stretches of time. So the necessity of constructing a practical identity gives you some reason to defer to your past plans, even when you prefer a different plan in the present and future. Honoring past plans is permissible when those plans play a role in constructing your practical identity.

Korsgaard's approach to rationality is rich and interesting and significantly different from the theory of approbative rationality we have been developing here. For instance, she thinks there is a tight connection between our actions and our practical identities—we need practical identities to distinguish actions from mere behaviors, but we can only construct our practical identities through our actions. Her approach is focused on action as the key component of practical reason, whereas we've been focused on preferences as the basic component. Comparing these approaches in any responsible detail would take us too far afield of the present task of trying to answer the sunk cost puzzle.

It is also not clear that the value of having a practical identity is sufficient to explain examples of intuitively permissible honoring of sunk costs. First, note that the integrity argument only applies to agents who need a practical identity so they can continue to act in the future. So it cannot explain why someone who has no future, like George, could have any reason to tie up his loose writing ends on his deathbed.

The integrity approach is also likely to lead to an overly conservative approach to rational planning. Consider another case:

Midlife Crisis: Lauren has dedicated most of her life to her legal career. She wakes up on the eve of her forty-fifth birthday no longer enamored of her job. She prefers to quit and set out on a new but undetermined course. She is confident she will never regret quitting but she will continue to have regrets if she stays. She starts to draft her resignation letter but pauses: if she's not a lawyer, she'll lose much of her practical identity. Is that a reason to stay?

It would be odd to say that Lauren ought to stay with her job because she should value having the identity she's constructed. She doesn't want to be a lawyer anymore! The mere fact that this is her identity just isn't important. The integrity argument goes too far in assuming we require these practical identities in order to serve as reasons for preferences and choices. While reasons from our practical identities can back our preferences, we do not always need such reasons. And sticking with an undesirable career because you have already let it shape who you are seems like a paradigm of irrational sunk cost reasoning. Weak Honoring explains this. The fact that Lauren has long preferred a law career is made irrelevant by the fact that she'd regret the career going forward.

9.8 Sticking to Your Plans

It is sometimes permissible to stick to your plans, even if you have changed your mind and even if you haven't gained or lost reasons. Temporal neutrality explains why—your remembered past preferences can license your present preferences and choices just as much as your anticipated future preferences. The mere fact that planning was done in the past is no reason to ignore it now. As I have argued in this chapter, the theory is more systematic and offers a better answer to the sunk cost puzzle than rivals. And while Weak Honoring (like Weak Forecasting) is an idealized principle, there are more nuanced variants like Balanced Honoring that, appropriately developed, offer a strategy for taking our past into account in our planning.

10

Neutrality and Life Extension

> But now you will blind with light the solitude that death has made; you will disturb that corner where I had thought I might lie safe for ever.
>
> W. B. Yeats, *Calvary*

10.1 The Lazarus Problem

In April of 2014 my tennis-playing, non-drinking, non-smoking, seemingly healthy fifty-seven-year-old father had a sudden heart attack. He survived the initial event, but the days that followed forced our family to confront some hard realities about his health. We spent a lot of time playing the "best possible outcome" game. What could we hope for from a cardiac catheterization? From triple bypass surgery? When could he leave intensive care? And to ourselves we each wondered—much more quietly—what will happen if he dies?

Death is, of course, inevitable. Long before my father's illness, I'd acknowledged that in the vague and emotionally detached way I acknowledge other events I assume are a long way off. And like many people, my views on death are informed by religious commitments. I'm a Catholic, and like many Christians, I practice a faith that teaches there is a hope for new life after death. Indeed, in the middle of every Sunday Mass, Catholics publicly affirm the Nicene Creed, which ends: "I look forward to the resurrection of the dead and the life of the world to come." I feel disingenuous every time we get to these lines, because, frankly, I'm not presently looking forward to the life of the world to come. I love *this* life. Am I being irrational when I nevertheless affirm the Creed?

The more you delve into theology of the afterlife, the weirder and less exciting it seems. St. Thomas Aquinas says we can look forward to contemplating God forever.[1] (He also purports to prove that heaven is perfectly spherical, it being the most fitting shape.[2]) The biblical book of Revelation insists we'll get to help build the new Jerusalem of gold and jewels. On most Christian accounts, we will get new, unalterable bodies. We may or may not have free will. We may or may not have families. It is strongly suggested that there will be a lot of hymn singing. One could be forgiven for not being excited about moving on into this state.

Despite all of this, can we rationally prefer an afterlife over annihilation? Some people (my parents included) think such questions are best left for speech acts in church or casual cocktail party philosophizing and best left *out* of hospital waiting rooms. But I think there are three reasons why we should confront the question soberly and directly, and we should deliberate about it in times of both health and crisis.

First, as I have argued throughout this book, even if we do not have any meaningful control over the relevant options, we can still express our rational capacities by deliberating about what we prefer. In fact, the last shred of agency available to us when faced with catastrophes like death is deciding how we will greet it and what we hope will come from it. So I think this is a topic where philosophy can not only offer comfort, it can give us back some of our humanity. Indeed, the medievals were so committed to this idea that they published *Ars Moriendi*—guidebooks for preparing for a good death throughout your life. We moderns are more likely to put off the questions, as a result finding ourselves unprepared for death and our institutions unprepared to counsel us.[3]

Second, as we've learned with other distant future planning problems in this book, it can be hard to appreciate the value of our different options if we *only* contemplate them from an emotional distance. Hospital waiting rooms and other places of crisis give us a different perspective on what's at stake. While our emotions can sometimes distract us from our reasons (as we saw in Chapter 8), they can also sometimes motivate us to a better grasp of them.

Finally—and as I will argue in this chapter—the problem we face in forming preferences about the spiritual afterlife is just one instance of a far more general planning problem: when can you rationally prefer that your life be extended in the face of radical change? Resurrection is one

[1] *Summa Theologica* 2-2:179–81. [2] Book II, Lectures 5 and 6 of *De Caelo*.
[3] I am grateful to Dr. Lydia Dugdale for discussion on this point.

potential radical change. But we can also face this problem when deciding our preferences about surviving radical psychological or physical change. For example:

> **The Big Sleep:** Peter and Pat Shaw were accomplished Australian scientists and inveterate planners. As they entered their eighties, they began experiencing the symptoms of age-related mental and physical decline. Their hearing and eyesight were failing, they were losing mental acuity, and Pat was suffering from high blood pressure. They joined a euthanasia organization called Exit International. One October morning, the Shaws sent their adult daughters out to walk along the Melbourne beach near their home. They hugged them, said goodbye, and took lethal doses of medication. In his suicide note, Peter offered his argument for ending his life: "Senility is setting in fast. My mind doesn't work as well or as quickly as it used to, and it is getting worse day by day . . . life is an effort. I am not afraid of dying but I am afraid of pain and incompetence . . . I look forward calmly to a sleep from which I will not awake."[4]

Peter Shaw didn't believe in a spiritual afterlife, but even if he had, he didn't want an extended life if it would be significantly different from what he currently valued in his life. In earlier writing on his decision to end his life he insisted, "Our reason for suicide . . . [is] quite likely just a sense of a life accomplished and coming to a conclusion."

Let's define an *afterlife* broadly to be any period of extended conscious existence after some irreversible radical change. The radical change might be death and resurrection. Or it might be profound psychological change, as accompanies the onset of dementia. Or it might be profound physical change, like losing the use of your limbs, your sight, or your hearing. The life after this radical change might be infinite (as in the spiritual afterlife) or finite. You might think the question of whether to prefer an afterlife to final death is obvious: assuming the new phase of existence is worthwhile, you should *obviously* prefer going on to expiring. But even assuming life could be worthwhile dealing with dementia and serious new physical limits, it isn't obvious Peter Shaw should want it.

[4] Julia Medew, "The Big Sleep," *Canberra Times*, January 1, 2016.

Artistic treatments of the biblical Lazarus raise a similar question for the value of a spiritual afterlife, depicting the resurrected saint as deeply ambivalent about leaving the tomb. In his play *Calvary*, William Butler Yeats has his recently resurrected Lazarus lament to Christ: "Now you will blind with light the solitude that death has made; you will disturb that corner where I thought I might lie safe forever."[5] In a famous sculpture at Oxford's New College Chapel, Jacob Epstein portrays Lazarus walking out of his tomb, his shroud falling away but his neck wrenched backward, staring longingly back at oblivion. In his song "Dig, Lazarus, Dig!" Australian rocker Nick Cave imagines immortal Lazarus wandering the streets of present-day New York, lamenting that he was never consulted about whether to remain dead.

The Lazarus problem is the problem of explaining when (if ever) it is prudentially rational to prefer an afterlife in our sense over annihilation. How does radical change weigh into or inhibit our rational planning? In this chapter, I'll lay out the three assumptions about afterlives, both the spiritual and the earthly. I'll consider different strategies for answering the Lazarus problem, each of which contends that one feature of afterlives is most significant to planning. I'll describe how temporal neutrality answers the problem, and argue that this strategy is more defensible than the alternatives. In particular, some currently trendy approaches to life extension contend that radical change gives you compelling reason to prefer death. As we'll see, temporal neutrality shows there are many scenarios where it is perfectly permissible to prefer going on.

10.2 Afterlives

Presumably the rational appeal of an afterlife depends on what that life would entail. There are three questions we tend to focus on when we're deliberating about afterlife preferences.

First: How different will the afterlife be from what presently gives your life value? Call this the *difference question*. It suggests related questions. In the process of undergoing the change, which of your present properties will you permanently lose? What properties will you permanently gain? You might think that the more intense the permanent change is, the

[5] Yeats (1996).

less reason you have to prefer the afterlife. This may be because you are engaging in personal discounting (though we raised issues for this back in Chapter 4). Or it may be, more straightforwardly, because you do not now value the way you anticipate you would live post-change.

Second: Would the afterlife be worthwhile for you while you are in it? Call this the *satisfaction question*. You might think that your reasons to prefer an afterlife depend on your confidence that it will be a good one. While some of your options come with guarantees of satisfaction (i.e., a heavenly afterlife), others require a bit of research. Are people generally satisfied with their lives if they lose the use of their limbs? If they survive a horrible burn? What cognitive capacities do you need to have the preferences relevant to rational planning?

Third: Can you accurately imagine now what it will be like in your afterlife? Call this the *phenomenological question*. You might think that you can only reason about the value of *your* afterlife if you can adequately envision what it will be like "from the inside."

The Lazarus problem is difficult because we seek answers to all three questions, and in many cases we cannot answer all three. The Shaws presumably could not imagine what it would be like "from the inside" to be dementia patients. Does that mean their planning was not rational? The theology of heaven (and hell) is wildly speculative. Believers cannot be confident what particular aspects of their personality, body, or social identities will be preserved in the process. Does that mean Christians are making an irrational leap when they affirm that they look forward to the life to come? And if you cannot answer the phenomenological or difference questions, can you get traction on the satisfaction question?

I think we often only need to consider one question—the satisfaction question—in order to form rational preferences about afterlives. Difference and phenomenology are irrelevant if we can answer the satisfaction question in other ways. And we can often answer the satisfaction question in other ways. So, I'll argue, the Lazarus problem is more tractable than you might imagine. I'll argue for this both indirectly and directly. Indirectly, I'll consider why some philosophers, bioethicists, and psychologists have thought the phenomenological and difference questions are relevant. I'll argue that their principles have implausible consequences if generalized to other kinds of rational planning. More directly, I'll propose a principle for answering the Lazarus problem based on a particular understanding of the satisfaction question. I will argue that this principle fits well with a more general model of rational planning, distilled from the Weak Forecasting principle in earlier chapters.[6]

10.3 Caring about Difference?

You might think that the value of an afterlife depends on the extent to which that life will match up with your current preferences and life plans. In *Being Mortal*, physician Atul Gawande argues that it is often irrational for patients to prolong their natural life if the life extension involves a significant departure from their present plans and values. He describes the planning problem his father faced near the end of his life:

> **Spinal Tumor:** Atmaram Gawande was a physician, an avid tennis player, and governor of his Rotary club district. In his late seventies, Gawande was diagnosed with an extensive spinal tumor. After a few years of living with symptoms, he faced the choice of getting surgery to remove the tumor or letting the cancer progress. The surgery carried a high risk of mortality. The cancer's progress would mean he'd soon become quadriplegic. Gawande's father preferred to get the surgery, because much of what currently made his life valuable would be lost if he became paralyzed.

Atul Gawande compares his father to another patient with a similar tumor who preferred to live with his tumor: "(Mr. Block) said that if he could still watch football on television and eat chocolate ice cream, that would be good enough for him. My dad didn't think that would be good enough for him at all. Being with people and interacting with them was what he cared about most . . . He couldn't accept a life of complete physical paralysis, of needing total care . . . 'Never,' he said. 'Let me die instead.' "[7]

Gawande thinks physicians should help patients deliberate about life extension by having frank conversations about what patients presently value in their lives and helping them determine if those values could be accommodated by any life-extending intervention they are entertaining. Gawande is a prominent example of a popular recent trend in medical

[6] I assume that it is possible for you to survive the changes that would be required to have an afterlife. But even if you doubt the afterlife is metaphysically possible, this is no barrier to forming preferences about it, as we saw in Chapters 5 and 7.

[7] Gawande (2014: 212).

ethics aimed at helping people plan more carefully about the length of their lives. In an October 2014 feature in *The Atlantic*, bioethicist Ezekiel Emanuel declared that he prefers to not live much longer than seventy-five. He gives his reasons: "American immortals may live longer than their parents, but they are likely to be more incapacitated. Does that sound very desirable? Not to me." A bit later: "By 75, creativity, originality, and productivity are pretty much gone for the vast, vast majority of us." And at the end: "What I am trying to do is delineate my views for a good life and make my friends and others think about how they want to live as they grow older. I want them to think of an alternative to succumbing to that slow constriction of activities and aspirations imperceptibly imposed by aging."[8]

We can agree from a moral and policy perspective that individuals should have the freedom to make decisions about their healthcare, while still wondering whether it is rational for individuals to deliberate in this way about how they want their lives to end. What theory of prudential rationality do Gawande and Emanuel have in mind when they give this advice? Their difference-focused arguments for not extending life seem to operate on a strongly present-biased planning strategy:

> **Present Preference Principle:** If you now prefer options like A over options like B, then it is now rationally permissible to prefer some future option like A over some future option like B.

Thus if, like the elder Gawande, you now reckon incapacitation as worse than death, it is rationally permissible to prefer a high-risk surgery rather than the certainty of future incapacitation.

The Present Preference principle offers some substantive guidance on what afterlife preferences are permissible, even if it doesn't tell you what you are required to prefer. In the spiritual afterlife case: if you now prefer sleeping to contemplating the divine, you may prefer death to heaven. So the principle has the benefit of issuing verdicts for other variants of the Lazarus problem.

The trouble is, the Present Preference principle is false. There are many cases where it seems irrationally short-sighted to evaluate our

[8] Ezekiel J. Emanuel, "Why I Hope to Die at 75," *The Atlantic*, October 2014.

future options based only on our present preferences. This is because our preferences frequently change over time. For example, for most of my early life, I despised curry in all of its forms. Then in 2015, after my stint in Singapore, my tastes rapidly changed. It is now one of my favorite meals. Suppose before my trip I was asked whether I'd like to commit in advance to a diet plan: Singaporean food or more Western-style dishes. It would have been irrational to commit to Western food based on my present preferences—these are preferences that I have every reason to believe are volatile, especially when traveling. What I should be more concerned with is whether I predict I'll be satisfied with my options *when I am on the trip*. At least, this is how an advocate of Strong Forecasting would approach the planning question. But even if we deny Strong Forecasting, we can still acknowledge that there are important alternatives to the present preference approach, namely principles like Weak Forecasting. And Gawande and Emanuel's proposals are far less interesting once you realize you are in no way rationally pressured to defer to your present preferences.

Back in Chapter 4, I cautioned against taking our knee-jerk patterns of egoistic concern too seriously in our rational planning. There is good reason to think these patterns exhibit bias, in particular the pattern of bias described by the Moral Valence Hypothesis. Relevant to Gawande and Emanuel's arguments, there is likewise good empirical evidence that we are biased when it comes to anticipating the effect of disability on our well-being. Indeed, there has been considerable work in social psychology on the so-called "disability paradox"—non-disabled people predict a significant decline in their quality of life were they to become disabled, but in fact many who are disabled report a quality of life that is comparable with the non-disabled.[9] For instance, able-bodied individuals tend to be willing to pay more to avoid disability than disabled individuals are willing to pay to regain the relevant function.[10] Various factors have been suggested as explaining these attitudes. Nefarious moral and social associations with disability limit our ability to project our "true self" into disability scenarios. We tend to focus on some features of a changed state while ignoring others that would be relevant. We underestimate our abilities to adapt.[11] What's the common feature in these explanations?

[9] Albrecht and Devlieger (1999). [10] Gilbert (2006: 166).
[11] Ubel et al. (2005).

They treat our deference to present preferences *as a bias* and recommend making crucial medical plans in ways that are more responsive to what our future preferences are likely to be.

10.4 Prioritizing Satisfaction

The present preference approach is generally a poor way to reason about your future preferences, and the mere difference between your present life and an afterlife is no reason in and of itself to discount the afterlife. What about the satisfaction assumption?

You might think that the spiritual afterlife puzzle and the medical afterlife puzzles are not analogous in one key respect. Most religious traditions assume the spiritual afterlife will be infinitely long once it begins, while the medical afterlives will offer only finite life extension. So if we focus on satisfaction, you might think that the infinite magnitude of a spiritual afterlife is a reason to prefer it to finitude, whereas for the medical afterlife cases, we should trade off the length of life extension with the amount of well-being we'd have at each time in the afterlife. The usual tactic in medical ethics involves calculating and comparing the Quality Adjusted Life Years (QALYs) for relevant options.

On this approach, we might solve the Lazarus problem by adopting the simple approach to calculating the value of a life which we surveyed in Chapter 2:

> **The Simple Approach for Life Extension:** It is rationally permissible (and perhaps rationally obligatory) to prefer some potential future state of affairs A over some potential future state of affairs B if A has greater aggregate expected well-being than B.

But there are serious problems with the simple approach to the Lazarus problem. As we saw in Chapter 2, this principle falls prey to versions of the single life repugnant conclusion. And it has especially strange implications when the options are infinitely long. Suppose, for instance, that hell isn't so bad—everyone who goes to hell spends an infinite amount of time there, but every day the torture and rest are spaced in such a way that the day leaves you (just barely) with a positive balance of well-being. The simple approach entails that it is rationally permissible to prefer this hell to any very happy but finite extension of your natural life. But it is not obvious that it is in your interest to go to this hell. It certainly isn't obligatory. Infinities add up in strange ways.[12]

I propose another, weaker principle for reasoning about life extension, one that harkens back to the Weak Forecasting discussion in Chapter 6. The original principle stated you may always prefer a path of no regret to one where you sometimes prefer you'd chosen otherwise, assuming you are fully informed of the relevant information (and not intrinsically irrational). But in this application, one of the states of affairs you are deliberating about is one in which you do not exist and therefore do not have any preferences at all, let alone any regrets. So we need to tweak the principle so it does not require preferences in every future state of affairs. Here is an option, familiar to us from the discussion of the suicide problem for Weak Forecasting:

> **Weak Forecasting for Life Extension:** If now and for every time you consciously exist, you have and will have all of the relevant information about your situation and the capacity to appreciate that information, then it is rationally permissible to prefer any option you will always affirm or be indifferent towards over an option that you will not always affirm or be indifferent towards (either because you will regret it or lack conscious existence).

We could further weaken it to require that you only anticipate usually affirming your decision, akin to the Balanced Forecasting principle. The appropriate threshold for how often you should be satisfied with your decision might be something we build into the theory of rationality or might be a feature that varies from person to person.

Idealized forecasting principles like this can guide us in answering the Lazarus problem. If you assume you'll always be satisfied with your spiritual afterlife, you have reason to prefer it to final death. If you assume you'll permanently adapt to your disability, you have reason to prefer to live with a spinal tumor than to die. The verdicts are admittedly weak— they only give you permission. Still they point to considerations ignored by the present preference approach. And presumably we think there should be more liberal rational permissions in difficult problems like this.

[12] See footnote 7 in Chapter 2.

10.5 Temporal Neutrality and Life Extension

But is reasoning about afterlives this easy? There are a few wrinkles, which, in the process of addressing them, will help us get more clear on how temporal neutrality advises us to think about life extension.

First, some philosophers contend that in the infinitely long afterlife case, temporal neutrality will entail that you should always prefer death to an infinite afterlife. For instance, Bernard Williams and Samuel Scheffler insist that there will inevitably come a point in any sufficiently long life when you should prefer to reach an end, since you will inevitably run out of projects worth valuing. According to Scheffler, "Our lives are so pervasively shaped by the understanding of them as temporally limited that to suspend that understanding would call into question the conditions under which we value our lives and long for their extension . . . Our collective understanding of the range of goals, activities, and pursuits that are available to a person, the challenges he faces, and the satisfactions that he may reasonably hope for are all indexed to (finite life) stages."[13] Our ability to find value in our life projects presupposes finitude. So any person who opted for an infinite afterlife could predict that, inevitably, they would come to regret their decision.

For my part, I am unpersuaded by the inevitable boredom arguments. I think they presuppose that the ways we get value in the infinite afterlife are similar to the ways we get value in our finite lives. They also presuppose we know what it will be like to be in such a scenario. I don't think we have any reason to be confident in either assumption. That said, Weak Forecasting explains why *if* Scheffler and Williams were right about inevitable boredom, there would be good reason not to hope for immortality.

Second, you might worry that the temporally neutral approach to life extension doesn't have the resources to handle cases of cognitive change. For instance:

> **Still Alice:** Alice is diagnosed with early-onset Alzheimer's disease.[14] She can either end her life in the next few months or allow her disease to progress. If her disease progresses, she'll lose most of her memories and presently defining personality traits. She'll become utterly

[13] Scheffler (2013: 95–6).
[14] This case is based on the central plot line of the 2014 film *Still Alice*.

dependent upon her family and hospital caregivers. Right now she prefers *not* to ever be dependent in this way. But she predicts that as the disease progresses, she will change so that dependency doesn't bother her.

Does the Weak Forecasting principle license Alice to go on?

There are two ways we can understand how Alice changes over the course of the disease, and neither way of understanding her change poses an irresistible problem for Weak Forecasting for Life Extension. First we might understand Alice as having the same preferences throughout her change, but losing information about her situation. In this interpretation, Alice's "latent" preference is that she not exist rather than be utterly dependent, but Alice is not aware that she is utterly dependent. In this interpretation, temporal neutrality does not license Alice to go on, since she has lost crucial information about her predicament. Weak Forecasting does not license anything when information is lost.

But there is another way to interpret Alice's change. Suppose she does not believe she will lose relevant information about what she is like, only that her preferences will change in the future and she does not want to be the person with the new preferences. For instance, now she finds it abhorrent to think she'll ever live in such a way where she is utterly dependent upon her family and hospital caregivers. But she also thinks as her disease progresses, her preferences will change such that she prefers dependence to death. And suppose that for at least a time after this change, she'll still have the basic relevant information about her situation, namely, she will be aware that she has become dependent. In this case, temporal neutrality licenses going on into the state that she (now) finds abhorrent.[15]

This interpretation of Alice's predicament parallels a case raised by Derek Parfit in *Reasons and Persons*: the Russian Nobleman problem.[16] Briefly: the nobleman is a young socialist who stands to inherit a fortune in a few years. He knows when he inherits the fortune, he will inevitably become a greedy capitalist. Does the fact that his preferences

[15] We can also imagine versions of Weak Forecasting that tolerate changes in the threshold for relevant information. For instance, the information that is relevant for a normally functioning adult might be significantly richer than the information that is relevant for a cognitively disabled adult.

[16] Parfit (1984: 327). I have simplified the case somewhat here.

will inevitably change give him compelling reason to plan now for satisfying the preferences in the life he rejects—the life of a greedy capitalist? And if so, is this a counterexample to temporal neutrality?

I don't see it as an objection, because the only good reason for thinking that the nobleman ought to bind his future self is that we think that his future preferences are intrinsically irrational or immoral. To test this, consider your evaluation of the *reverse* Russian Nobleman case. A greedy and self-interested youth predicts that as he gets older, he will inevitably become more generous with his giving, develop more socialist politics, and become less materialistic. The young, conservative nobleman finds such a life abhorrent. Are we still inclined to think it rationally permissible (or even obligatory) for the young nobleman to bind his future self to his present plans? My inclination is to think the nobleman would be irrational to bind himself in this way—he ought to ensure that his preferences are satisfied *even when* he becomes a bleeding-heart middle-aged nobleman.[17] Indeed, the Russian Nobleman case and its reverse are excellent examples of the moral valence bias in egoistic concern.

We can evaluate the second interpretation of the Alzheimer's case along similar lines. If you think the early-onset Alzheimer's patient should prefer not to go on, you should press to ask why. Is it because you think there is something intrinsically irrational or immoral with preferring a life of profound dependence? Weak Forecasting could be overridden by such considerations. Such a position, I'd add, reflects an unjustifiably narrow view on the value of a life. Finally, note that even setting aside the cognitive decline cases, there is little reason to believe that many afterlives we deliberate about are intrinsically irrational or immoral.

The theory of temporal neutrality (and in particular this version of Weak Forecasting) offers an informative—if idealized—strategy for reasoning about our preferences for life extension. And it does not fall prey to the counterexamples that plague the simple approach and the present preference approach. But before we rest the case for Weak Forecasting, we have one more variable to consider. Does the difficulty we have in imagining what afterlives will be like pose any threat to rationally deliberating about them? Should we pay any attention to the phenomenological question?

[17] Thanks to an audience at NUS for discussion of this point.

10.6 Caring about Phenomenology?

Approbative rationality demands that our preferences be based on appropriate reasons. And we can (and often should) take our anticipated preference changes into account when planning for the future—indeed, that's a lesson from other chapters of this book. But you might think this lesson is particularly hard to apply in these cases, because a non-disabled person cannot know what it would be like for him to live as a quadriplegic. The Shaws had no idea what it would be like to live in the advanced stages of dementia. Knowing that other patients report satisfaction in such lives is not the same as knowing what it would be like to live in *your* afterlife.

In a recent book, *Transformative Experience*, L. A. Paul proposes that phenomenological ignorance creates challenges for our usual approaches to rational planning.[18] Suppose you were assured of some great but indescribable value in a potential afterlife. Does that make it rational to assign some great value to the afterlife option? Paul contends that it does not. Consider a thought experiment she gives in her opening chapter:

> **Vampires:** You are given the opportunity to become a vampire. No one can describe to you accurately what it is like to be a vampire, though you can get some hints. You'll prefer drinking animal blood to martinis. You'll prefer nights roaming the streets to warm summer beach days. You'll generally avoid stakes, garlic, and crosses. What you are promised is that everyone who becomes a vampire highly values their new and transformed state.

Is it rational to prefer to become a vampire? Absent important phenomenological knowledge, Paul argues that you cannot, in your current mortal state, assign a value to the vampire outcome.[19] If phenomenological ignorance precludes assigning a value in the vampire scenario, it ought to preclude assigning a value in the other analogous afterlife scenarios.

Paul's target is expected utility theory: the theory that a rational agent should decide what to do by calculating the value and probability for each possible option her actions might bring about. But Paul's general strategy implies a principle that applies to other frameworks for rational planning, including the temporal neutrality framework developed here. Paul seems to endorse a *projection requirement* on rational planning: you

[18] Paul (2014). [19] See Chapter 1 of Paul (2014).

can determine the prudential value of some future states of affairs A and B only if you are able to predict what it will be like to experience those states of affairs. The projection requirement combined with the phenomenological ignorance assumption would raise a serious challenge for forming rational preferences about afterlives, since we are rarely in a position to know what life after radical change will be like "from the inside." At best, we can model it based on reports from others. Paul motivates such a requirement by arguing that we value authenticity in our future planning: "What you care about when making a decision about your own personal future, is not the third personal descriptive knowledge that you will have certain properties in the future, but your experience-based first personal knowledge of what it will be like for you to have these properties. In other words, you care what it will be like for *you* to experience *your* future, because you want to determine *your* preferences in terms of *your* expected subjective values."[20]

The projection requirement entails that we cannot use expected utility theory to plan around more common transformative events, like deciding to become a parent, go to war, or undergo a radical medical procedure. For these reasons alone you might be suspicious that it is too strong. At the very least Paul owes us a theory of error for why we often seem to approach such decisions as though we are making them rationally.

Is the projection requirement independently well-motivated? Paul's Vampires case is strikingly similar to the Russian Nobleman problem we surveyed in the previous section—informed by childhoods full of horror films, we are likely inclined to think there is something intrinsically immoral or irrational about being a vampire. This almost certainly shades our judgments about our ability to rationally prefer the transformation.

Moreover (as Paul acknowledges) the projection requirement will fail to give defensible verdicts if we apply it in third personal cases. In Chapter 8, I argued that it is evidence against a principle of rationality if it issues split verdicts in its self-regarding and other-regarding applications. Would an impartial spectator endorse a projectability constraint on rational planning? Clearly not. Suppose President Obama cares about the Deaf community, though he has no way of knowing what it is like to live as a Deaf person or participate in Deaf culture. A law is proposed

[20] Paul (2014: 109). Emphases in the original.

which would make new funds available for Deaf orchestral performances. Obama has reason to believe that the program, if instituted, would satisfy preferences of many individuals in the Deaf community. Does the fact that Obama doesn't have phenomenological knowledge of how the preferences will be satisfied pose any challenge to his ability to rationally prefer that the law be enacted? No. All that matters is that the group he cares about will be satisfied in the scenario where the law is enacted. In the case of other-regarding preferences, phenomenological ignorance is widespread. But it is no barrier to rational planning as long as we have other, indirect ways of knowing whether preferences are satisfied. And if we desire to have principles that generalize across self-regarding and other-regarding planning, then we shouldn't adopt a projectability constraint. The satisfaction question is important when we are deliberating about afterlives; the phenomenological question is only important insofar as projection can help us estimate satisfaction. And often, as we see in the paradox of disability cases, projection is a poor guide to satisfaction.

10.7 Better Retirements, Better Deaths

My father had triple bypass surgery in May of 2014. After some frightening post-surgery complications, he recovered, and he is now a vigorous sixty-year-old. There is a tendency to think that questions of rational religious belief are in principle unanswerable or significantly more difficult than other sorts of rational planning questions. If I have convinced you of anything in this chapter, I hope it is that this is not the case—a sufficiently powerful theory of rational planning can help us not only make better retirement decisions, but also more clearly formulate and precisely respond to our bigger existential predicaments.

In the final chapter, we will apply the theory to perhaps the biggest existential question of all—given the finitude of our (earthly) life, how can we rationally believe that our projects have meaning? As with the Lazarus problem, the theory of temporal neutrality can also give us guidance on the relationship between time and meaning.

11

Neutrality and Meaning

(Our past) is the period of our time which is sacred and dedicated, which has passed beyond all human risks and is removed from Fortune's sway . . . It cannot be disturbed or snatched from us: it is an untroubled, everlasting possession.

Seneca, *On the Shortness of Life*

11.1 The Ecclesiastes Problem

In 1879, at age fifty, Leo Tolstoy was an internationally celebrated literary genius. He led a prosperous family with a well-appointed estate in Samara. He was at the height of his creative powers. And he was contemplating suicide. While untreated depression and religious obsession may be part of the explanation of his crisis, his despair was also philosophical. In particular, he was caught in the grip of an argument that all of his projects, regardless of their success, were now and always would be meaningless. In his *Confessions*, Tolstoy writes:

My question, the one that brought me to the point of suicide . . . was a most simple one . . . what will come of what I do today or tomorrow? . . . is there any meaning in my life which will not be annihilated by the inevitable death that awaits me? . . . I could not attribute any rational meaning to a single act, let alone to my whole life. I simply felt astonished that I had failed to realize this from the beginning . . . Today or tomorrow sickness and death will come (and they had already arrived) to those dear to me, and to myself, and nothing will remain other than the stench and the worms. Sooner or later my deeds, whatever they may have been, will be forgotten and will no longer exist. What is all the fuss about then? How can a person carry on living and fail to perceive this? That is what is so astonishing! It is only possible to go on living while you are intoxicated with life; once sober it is impossible not to see that it is all a mere trick, and a stupid trick![1]

[1] Tolstoy (1987: Chapter 4).

Tolstoy's worry is not new. For instance, the book of Ecclesiastes in the Bible is devoted primarily to reminding the reader that in the great scope of history, your efforts are all pointless. "Vanity of vanities! All is vanity! What gain is there for man in all his toil that he toils under the sun? A generation goes and a generation comes, but the earth endures forever" (Chapter 1). "There is no remembrance of the wise, as with the fool, forever. Since in the days to come, all will be forgotten. Yes, the wise dies like the fool" (Chapter 3). As with other books in the Wisdom tradition (like Job), the author of Ecclesiastes raises a fascinating puzzle . . . and then does nothing to solve it for us.

Nihilism is the view that our lives and all of the activities that occur within them are meaningless. Different paths might lead you to nihilism. For instance, you might think the very concept of "meaningfulness" as a kind of enduring value is incoherent. Another path to nihilism focuses on the inevitable pain and disappointment that accompany our lives. Still another path to nihilism is spatial; we are so small and insignificant compared with the vastness of the cosmos.[2] But the author of Ecclesiastes and Tolstoy both find themselves in the grips of a distinctively *temporal* argument for nihilism. The argument is based on two assumptions:

The Temporal Argument for Nihilism

(1) The meaningfulness of an activity at a time depends upon it making a permanent difference in the world. (The Permanence principle)
(2) Nothing we can do will make a permanent difference in the world.
C. Nothing we can do has meaning now.

Each premise is controversial, though most of the interesting philosophical work is done by (1)—which we might call *the permanence principle*. In this closing chapter, I'll deploy the theory of temporal neutrality to answer the Temporal Argument for Nihilism. And in the process, I will identify a strain of time bias in contemporary work on meaning and argue that it is unmotivated. But before turning to these applications, why would anyone find Premises (1) or (2) of the Temporal Argument for Nihilism appealing in the first place?

[2] For discussion see Kahane (2014).

11.2 Meaning as a Form of Value

To understand Premise (1), we should first get more clear on the concept of meaning in play. And it is, admittedly, a slippery concept. Often we speak about "meaning" as what a word, depiction, or symbol refers to. But here we are not worried about what an event or life might represent. Rather we understand the meaning or meaningfulness of an activity as a form of value it has at a time that is distinct from the pain or pleasure it conveys at that time. Here I'll use both "meaning" and "meaningfulness" interchangeably to pick out this kind of value. Consider three cases of this kind of valuing, which will give us concrete examples of the framework to come:

Abstract Expressionism: Sam is now at the Tate Modern, studying Mark Rothko's painting *Black on Maroon*. The experience of viewing the painting gives him slight pleasure, about the same as the pleasure he would receive from walking into a room with bold wallpaper. But Sam also has been an avid follower of abstract expressionism, and this is the first Rothko work he has seen in person. He knows that Rothko committed suicide at the height of his career, and Sam has a close friend who has also been struggling with depression. Sam now finds a great deal of meaning in studying the painting.

El Capitan: Blake is now on a solo hike in Yosemite National Park. He arrives near the base of El Capitan just as the sun is setting. The chromatic changes on the rock exhilarate him, giving a sensation akin to speeding down a roller coaster. He also suddenly feels overcome with gratitude for the experience and the distinctive beauty of the place. He finds a great deal of meaning in the experience of being at El Capitan in this moment.

Fatherhood: Richard is now celebrating the second birthday of his son, Freddie. He remembers a night around the time Freddie first came home from the hospital, when Freddie woke crying and Richard went to comfort him. At the time, the experience of soothing Freddie was painful—father and son were exhausted. When he thinks back on that night, he feels a bit of sympathetic pain for his sleep-deprived past self. And he realizes the event was deeply meaningful—it was the real moment when he transitioned to fatherhood.

In the first two cases, an agent assigns meaning to a present experience. In the third case, the meaning is assigned to an experience that is already in the past. Using these cases, we can start to develop a framework for understanding meaning as a form of value. The framework makes five assumptions.

First, meaningfulness is typically *distinct* from pleasure: the above cases are plausible examples of agents who assign both some (possibly negative) hedonic value to the experiences and some other value over and above it.[3] Note that nothing in this chapter depends on the more controversial thesis that there are two fundamentally distinct dimensions of value—hedonic and non-hedonic. If what is being classified as "meaningfulness" here can be subsumed under a hedonic framework, then the arguments will stand—they'll just be targeting a more sophisticated concept of hedonic value compared with a more basic form of hedonic value.

Second, meaningfulness is *atomistic*: we can assign meaningfulness to events of almost any duration within our lives. This assumption puts me at odds with philosophers like Robert Nozick, who assume that meaningfulness can only be assigned to the maximal limits of an entire life.[4] Still, I think this makes sense of an important way we talk about meaningfulness as attaching to particular experiences (as in the cases surveyed). Further, it avoids the unwelcome Solonian result of not being able to deem anything in your life meaningful while it is yet incomplete.

Third, the pursuit of meaning is *self-interested*: meaning contributes a kind of prudential value to a life or activity. That is, we need not think such value is purely moral or aesthetic. Related to this, we can form prudentially rational or irrational preferences about potentially meaningful events.

Fourth, meaningfulness is *commensurable* with pleasure: we can and often do trade more pleasurable options for more meaningful ones and vice versa. For instance, I may become a parent knowing that it

[3] It is an interesting question whether this non-hedonic value can be negative—for instance, whether some experiences can destroy meaning. I think it is a category worth identifying, but I won't try to argue for it here.

[4] Nozick (1981: 594). Susan Wolf thinks meaningful fulfillment is something properly ascribed to lives, but is silent on whether it can only be ascribed to a life fully lived. Wolf (2010). See Baumeister et al. (2013) for psychological research indicating that we attribute meaningfulness to fully integrated lives.

will increase my net future suffering but also vastly increase the net meaningfulness of my future experiences. Or you may decide that however meaningful the new Philip Glass opera is, the experience isn't worth the headache you'll inevitably endure afterward.

Finally, meaningfulness assignments depend on extrinsic facts in a way that pleasure assignments do not. Let's say that an assignment of value is *intrinsic* to an event if the value does not depend in any important way on facts outside of the event.[5] The vast majority of our assignments of meaning are *extrinsic*: they depend on facts about how a particular event relates to other facts about our lives, our culture, the environment, and how our projects relate to those of other people and other times. Indeed, some philosophers and psychologists define meaningfulness in such a way that assignments of meaning must be extrinsic. Nozick, for instance, assumes meaningfulness is explicitly relational.[6] Baumeister and his co-authors define meaning assignments as follows: "meaning itself is not personal but rather cultural. It is like a large map or web, gradually filled in by the cooperative work of countless generations. An individual's meaningfulness may be a personally relevant section of that giant, culturally created and culturally transmitted map."[7] For this reason, Baumeister theorizes that we often better appreciate the meaningfulness of an event after we have experienced it.

It will help in the arguments to come if we are even more precise. For any event E, the meaningfulness of E depends (partially or fully) on the meaningfulness of some fact or set of facts F that is extrinsic to E. We'll call facts of the F sort *connection facts*. The Abstract Expressionism and Fatherhood cases are clearly cases of extrinsic assignment of meaning. The meaning Sam assigns to studying the painting depends on the meaningfulness of contemporary expressionism and the meaningfulness of his personal relationships. The meaning Richard assigns to soothing his child is connected to cultural facts about the meaningfulness of parenthood. While El Capitan might seem like a case of an event being intrinsically meaningful, it is more plausible to think that Blake's epiphany

[5] To keep things tidy, we will assume that facts about when the event occurred and whether it is past, present, or future count as intrinsic to the event itself. But this does get us into tricky territory with the metaphysics of time—in particular the A-theory/B-theory debate.

[6] Nozick (1981: 599). [7] Baumeister et al. (2013: 506).

is importantly related to his beliefs about the value of the environment or consciously inaccessible facts about how this experience relates to other valuable ones in his life. While background beliefs and assumptions determine how we assign meaningfulness to events, we may not always be aware of how our valuing depends on these connection facts.

With this framework for understanding meaningfulness, we can understand the motives behind the Temporal Argument for Nihilism—in particular, Premise (1).

11.3 Future Bias about Meaning

Why think that for your activities to be meaningful, they must make a permanent difference to the world? Why isn't it enough to be a poor player who struts and frets an hour upon the stage and then is heard no more? As we saw in Tolstoy and Ecclesiastes, the Permanence principle is implicitly assumed. Nozick makes it more explicit in his discussion of nihilism, writing: "Death wipes you out. Dead, you are no longer around—around here at any rate—and if there is nowhere else you'll be (heaven, hell, with the white light) then all that will be left of you is your effects, leaving traces. People do seem to think it important to continue to be around somehow. The root notion seems to be this one: it shouldn't *ever* be as if you had never existed at all. A significant life leaves its mark on the world. A significant life is, in some sense, permanent; it makes a permanent difference to the world—it leaves traces. To be wiped out completely, traces and all, goes a long way toward destroying the meaning of one's life."[8]

The motivation for the Permanence principle comes from two assumptions. First, that meaning is extrinsic in the way described in the previous section. And second, that we are (or ought to be) future-biased about meaning. You are *future-biased about meaning* if you think the only connection facts that could contribute to the meaning of your present activities and experiences are future connection facts. Hence Nozick's idea that we need to leave traces to connect us with future generations.

[8] Nozick (1981: 582).

As we did with previous time biases, we can raise two questions about time and meaning. The first is descriptive: are we in fact disposed to be future-biased about meaning? The second is normative: should we be future-biased about meaning? And, as with other cases (like the debate about egoistic concern back in Chapter 4), we should assume the normative question presupposes a positive answer to the descriptive question. Nobody that I am aware of defends the revolutionary hypothesis that we should be future-biased about meaning even though we are, in fact, disposed to be future-neutral.

The limited philosophical discussion of future bias about meaning has proceeded using the method of thought experiments. For instance, consider your judgment about two related "sci fi" examples. The first comes from Samuel Scheffler. Scheffler is interested in how our valuing depends on our assumptions about future generations. He offers this case:

> **Doomsday:** Suppose you knew that, although you yourself would live a normal lifespan, the earth would be completely destroyed thirty days after your death in a collision with a giant asteroid.[9]

Scheffler argues that facing such a scenario we would find it very difficult to find meaning in our present activities. We would of course fear for what the scenario means for our lives. We'd worry that more long-term goal-oriented projects (like curing cancer) will have been in vain. But we will also face significant difficulty finding meaning in less goal-oriented projects, like appreciating art or achieving philosophical understanding.[10] Why would these activities lose value? Presumably it is because they would no longer be connected in any way with humanity's future. This theme is explored in much contemporary science fiction, including novels like *The Children of Men* (P. D. James) and *The Last Policeman* (Ben H. Winters).

Compare the typical judgment about the Doomsday scenario to another scenario, one suggested by Seana Shiffrin:

> **Fabrication:** Suppose we discovered that some ludicrous science-fiction conspiracy story was true—something like the Scientology myth—but occurring much more recently. Very different aliens created us and deposited us here around 150 years ago, left misleading

[9] Scheffler (2013: 18). [10] Scheffler (2013: 42–3).

evidence, and implanted effective but false myths about our personal, social, and biological histories.[11]

Both Scheffler and Shiffrin think that the Doomsday scenario poses a much greater threat to our ability to assign meaning in our lives than the Fabrication scenario.[12] In comparing the Doomsday and Fabrication scenarios, Shiffrin says: "it is especially hard to shake off the issues about deception [in Fabrication] . . . The scenario would certainly be distressing but, I think, mainly for those reasons . . . the fact that we lacked a true collective history, I think, would not be *as* distressing as the lack of a collective future."[13] And a bit later: "part of what matters most is not simply being a part of human (or rational) history and sustaining value through time, but doing so in a particular future-directed way."[14]

Scheffler and Shiffrin think that because Doomsday poses a much greater threat than Fabrication to our ability to find meaning, our meaning depends much more on future connections than past ones. Hence meaning is future-biased. Strict future bias about meaning would require connection facts to be future.

11.4 From Future Bias to the Permanence Principle

We'll return to these thought experiments in Section 11.8. But for now, let's grant that we are future-biased about meaning. Future bias gets us to a version of the Permanence principle by way of a regress problem. Unless our activities are part of a chain of events that makes a permanent difference to the world, there isn't anything to guarantee their meaning. More precisely, for any event E:

The Regress Argument for Permanence

(1) E is meaningful only if it is connected to some other event F that is meaningful. (Extrinsicness)
(2) F must occur after E. (Strict Future Bias about Meaning)
(3) For F to be meaningful, it must be connected to some other event G that is meaningful.

[11] Shiffrin (2013: 156). The name for the case is mine. [12] Scheffler (2013: 196).
[13] Shiffrin (2013: 157). [14] Shiffrin (2013: 158).

(4) G must occur after F . . . [Repeat (1)–(3)]

C. So if E is meaningful then it must be part of a chain of connected meaningful events extending infinitely into the future.[15]

An example makes the argument more vivid. Suppose Sam is at the Tate, viewing the Rothko painting and wondering whether this is a meaningful activity. He might reason as follows. Studying this painting could only be meaningful if abstract expressionism continues to be meaningful for the next hundred years. What would it take for abstract expressionism to remain meaningful for the next century? Well, it would require that even after the era of abstract expressionism ends it would have evolved into a new and related form of meaningful art. What would it take for that new form of art to be meaningful? The demand for future extrinsic connection facts keeps pushing Sam further and further into the future in search of meaning.

11.5 From Permanence to Nihilism

Future bias and meaning's dependence on extrinsic facts together get us to a version of the Permanence principle. Once we grant this version of the Permanence principle, we are in trouble, because if we project far enough into the future, we fail to find meaningful connections. At some point in the (hopefully distant) future environmental degradation, mass human extinction, or the heat death of the universe will mean there is nothing meaningful to which our lives will connect. Nobody will be around to make or appreciate art. There will be no family life. El Capitan will be space dust. Inevitably the domino series of meaning connections we've set up will come tumbling down. The realization that far enough out there are no connection facts combined with our version of the Permanence principle commits us to nihilism.[16]

We might, in response to the nihilist argument, decide to give up looking for meaning wholesale. Once we realize that none of our activities or experiences could achieve it, we should just focus on getting other

[15] Nozick (1981: Chapter 6) discusses a different regress problem for meaning, connected to the demand for ever broader contexts in which to situate a meaningful life.

[16] Mark Johnston calls this consequence of Scheffler's view the "Ponzi condition." See "Is Life a Ponzi Scheme?" *Aeon*, January 2, 2014.

kinds of value in our lives. This is, in effect, a kind of nihilism—but not the despairing variety we get from Tolstoy.

Even though this form of nihilism might be something we can live with, it would be nice to have other options for blocking the argument. In the remainder of this chapter I will consider two different strategies that have been suggested to reject one or another of the premises. The first—meaning subjectivism—resists the regress argument by insisting that meaning does not depend on any further extrinsic facts but rather only present desires. The second—heavenly optimism—blocks Premise (2) of the Temporal Argument for Nihilism by positing that our activities might be connected to an eternal afterlife of one sort or another. Both strategies fail. At the end of the chapter I'll suggest a better strategy for resisting nihilism—temporal neutrality about meaning. Temporal neutrality resists the Permanence principle by denying future bias about meaning, thereby blocking the regress argument.

11.6 Subjectivism about Meaning?

Richard Taylor, in a popular essay on the meaning of life, suggests that we avoid nihilism by denying the assumption that meaning depends on extrinsic connections. In particular, he criticizes the assumption that meaningfulness depends on accomplishment. He opens his discussion with a version of the Temporal Argument for Nihilism:

> If the builders of a great and flourishing ancient civilization could somehow return now to see archaeologists unearthing the trivial remnants of what they had once accomplished with such effort—see the fragments of pots and vases, a few broken statues, and such tokens of another age and greatness—they could indeed ask themselves what the point of it all was, if this is all it finally came to... What was it all worth, if this is the final result?[17]

According to Taylor, instead of worrying about whether our activities contribute to the future, we can just will for them to be meaningful now. Our activities can be meaningful simply because we desire them. And if we can will our activities to have meaning while we pursue them, then impermanence is no problem. The subjectivist solves the Ecclesiastes problem with a personal attitude adjustment.

[17] Taylor (2000: 332).

But can we just manufacture meaningfulness? Subjectivism would seem to license some plans that seem straightforwardly irrational. For example:

> **Blades of Grass:** Denise spends an hour every afternoon meticulously counting blades of grass in her yard and recording the count in a notebook. She doesn't get a lot of pleasure from the activity. Indeed, all of the stooping, sweating, and bug bites cause her discomfort. But she has determined that it is worth the sacrifice, because she has decided that blade counting is a very meaningful activity.

Regardless of what Denise thinks, counting blades of grass is not a meaningful activity. Why? Because it is pointless—it does not contribute in any way to anything outside itself. It does not connect Denise with other people or with culture. While it brings her out in nature, it doesn't cause her to appreciate it or understand it in any deep way. It isn't worth her toil and sweat, and no change in her attitude could make it worth it.

Subjectivism also trivializes what are, for most of us, very difficult planning problems. When should we trade pleasure for meaning? For instance, should I become a parent? My life going forward will be more painful for a period, but also potentially more meaningful. This is a question that requires research, soul searching, and accurately forecasting my preferences. It requires hard thinking about the meaningfulness of family life and the generation that will come after my own. The subjectivist has an easy answer—as long as I think I will keep wanting to be a parent, the meaningfulness I manufacture will outweigh the sacrifice. The only planning question I need to answer is whether I think I will desire to be a parent once I become one. Family planning shouldn't be impossible, as I argued in the previous chapter. But it also shouldn't be this easy. I prefer to keep the extrinsicness assumption because I think meaningfulness is often a value we pursue, not one that we manufacture for ourselves. So while in earlier chapters I remained relatively agnostic about the kinds of value that figure into our well-being, here I sympathize with philosophers who think meaningfulness must have an objective dimension.[18]

Finally, we might worry that the subjectivist approach narrows the category of meaningful activities too much. For instance, it seems

[18] For instance, Wolf (2010).

meaningfulness can be ascribed to activities we do not love or desire. Sam might not love looking at the Rothko painting and contemplating the nature of depression, but the activity might be meaningful for him nevertheless, because it gives him insight into valuable ways that art helps victims of depression express their turmoil.

11.7 Heavenly Optimism?

Other philosophers have looked to religion to block Premise (2) of the Temporal Argument for Nihilism.[19] William Lane Craig promotes a version of the argument in his book *Reasonable Faith*. In the context of offering a popular Christian apologetic he writes:

> Mankind is a doomed race in a dying universe. Because the human race will eventually cease to exist, it makes no ultimate difference whether it ever did exist.... The contributions of the scientist to the advance of human knowledge, the researches of the doctor to alleviate pain and suffering, the efforts of the diplomat to secure peace in the world, the sacrifices of good people everywhere to better the lot of the human race—all these come to nothing. In the end they don't make one bit of difference, not one bit. *And because our lives are ultimately meaningless, the activities we fill our lives with are also meaningless.*[20]

Craig contends that the only way out of this nihilism is belief in "God and immortality." We need God to supply objective standards and purpose and immortality to satisfy the Permanence principle.

But the religious turn is a poor response to the Temporal Argument for Nihilism for (at least) two reasons. First, Craig's heavenly solution suggests that atheists or those who are not confident there is an afterlife shouldn't be able to find meaning in their lives. Craig is happy to accept this odious consequence of the view, but I take it as a reductio of any theory of meaning if it deprives many well-intentioned people of having meaning simply on the basis of their eschatological views.

Second, it is not clear on most pictures of the afterlife that anyone there or then will identify with any of our earthly activities. Recall from the previous chapter, many orthodox conceptions of the spiritual afterlife assume it is radically different from our earthly life. There is little reason to

[19] Nozick solves a similar version of the regress problem by postulating a limitless God. Nozick (1981: Chapter 6).

[20] Craig (1994: 73). Emphasis added.

think there will be art movements or hiking trails in the heaven promised by major world religions. And there is little reason to think the morally transformed individuals enjoying the afterlife will understand or care about the ways we filled our time in this life. So while the afterlife might be permanent, it couldn't supply the right connections to any of our earthly activities to make them meaningful.

11.8 Temporal Neutrality about Meaning

We shouldn't be nihilists. We won't secure meaning in ourselves or in heaven. Happily there is another route to rejecting the Temporal Argument for Nihilism. The Permanence principle only looks appealing if you are future-biased about meaning. We can reject it by instead adopting temporal neutrality. You are *temporally neutral about meaning* if you think connection facts can be drawn from any time in the past, present, or future.

Recall from Section 11.3 that the philosophical motivations for future bias about meaning rested largely on our different reactions to the Doomsday and Fabrication thought experiments. One defect of these thought experiments is that they both ask us to imagine scenarios where many of our ordinary beliefs about the past and future turn out to have been radically mistaken. It is likely that we have stronger emotional responses to scenarios where we discover we have been wrong in a future prediction than cases where we discover we have been wrong about a past assumption, since mistakes in future predictions tend to have graver consequences.

But if we remove the element of surprise from the thought experiments, it is less clear there is any basis for future bias about meaning. For example, people often fantasize about what it would be like to live during a different time, experiencing the cultures and practices that would exist then. Presumably we think there would be many opportunities deep in the past and the future when we could pursue meaningful lives. Consider another thought experiment:

> **Choose Your Own Adventure:** At the start of time, God offers you a choice of which period of human history to live out your life in. You can pick to live somewhere near the beginning of human civilization, somewhere in the middle, or you can choose to live at the end.

> Regardless of what you choose, God assures you a life filled with opportunities for interesting friendships, intellectual questions, fine meals, the appreciation of nature, and the like.[21]

Would it be a mistake to choose to live towards the end of humanity, rather than somewhere in the beginning or middle? If you are future-biased about meaning, then it would be a terrible mistake to choose to live at the end: such a life would be devoid of important sources of value. At the very least, if you chose to live at the end, then many potentially meaningful activities would tend to matter far less than if you had chosen to live in the middle or beginning.

But this isn't realistic as a psychological posit or normative requirement. For some of us, at least, the prospect of living at the end would be very attractive because in key ways your activities could matter *more*. Consider the prospect of a life at the end of human history. From this privileged perspective, you might write the review of all we had accomplished and all we ever were—to survey, in a sense, humankind itself in all of its glory and ignominy. Even if there is sadness when valuable things come to an end, their ending does evoke a sense of importance. As in Greek tragedy, general awfulness is compatible with a deep sense of things mattering, especially when this allows one to achieve a grand perspective on what has transpired and why. A life at the end of humanity need not be devoid of meaning; for some people it could be immensely meaningful. Preston Greene calls this disposition to prefer appearing at the end of stories the "memorialist's impulse."[22]

Not everyone will share the memorialist's impulse. You might instead identify more with what Greene calls the "activist's impulse." Activists are people who care deeply about shaping the future for the better. It is compatible with this impulse that you'd have little patience for thinking about the past. Most of what matters to activists may focus solely on their contributions to projects that extend into the future, and they may care little for how their projects fit with traditions that extend into the past. Those that feel the activist's impulse more than the memorialist's impulse may choose a life towards the beginning of human civilization,

[21] I am grateful to Preston Greene for developing this case and the corresponding argument with me.

[22] Greene (MS).

in an attempt to maximize their potential impact on the future. For them, a life at the beginning of human civilization may contain more meaning.

Whether you are more engaged by the memorialist's or activist's impulse is probably a matter of the particular sorts of projects that you have come to care about. In any event, none of these impulses appear alien or are ruled out by deep facts about what matters to us. And yet future bias about meaning is difficult to square with the memorialist's impulse. This is reason to think future bias about meaning is unmotivated.

There are also, as we'd suspect, good arguments from the Success and Non-Arbitrariness principles against the rational permissibility of this kind of future bias. Here is the Non-Arbitrariness Argument: Just as there is no non-arbitrary reason for systematically distinguishing past and present hedonic experiences, there is no non-arbitrary reason to systematically prefer being connected with future generations of humanity rather than past ones. Different kinds of activities and personal tastes motivate us to look for meaningful connections with the future, the past, the near, and the far.

Here is the Success Argument: Just as hedonic future bias and near bias can lead you to have a less valuable life, so can future bias about meaning. The reasoning here is more blunt—unless you are temporally neutral about meaning, you won't be able to have *any* meaning in your activities, since future bias leads to nihilism.

How does temporal neutrality escape the regress problem from Section 11.4? While the meaning of an experience depends on its connection with another meaningful experience, that connection can just as well be a *past* connection as a future one. This means that it is possible for meaning connections to be mutually dependent: some event E's meaning depends on some future meaningful event F, and F's meaning in turn depends on its connection with the past meaningful event E. An example will make the solution more vivid:

Endangered Language: Ainu is a Japanese dialect spoken by members of the Ainu ethnic group on the island of Hokkaido. There are currently about one hundred native speakers of the language, and it will likely not exist in a generation. Ainu has a rich history: as early as the 1800s it was the predominant language of the ethnic group. An Ainu man in 1900 might find meaning in studying this language alongside Japanese because it connects him with his contemporaries and because

> he assumes his children and grandchildren will inherit the tradition. An Ainu man in 2016 might find meaning in studying the language only because it connects him with his ancestors, including the Ainu man of 1900. He has no reason to think anyone in the future will care about the tradition.[23]

The Ainu speakers form a temporally closed circuit of meaning. This kind of mutual meaning dependence is perfectly coherent, and it avoids the regress problem. But it requires temporal neutrality.

11.9 Meaning and Vulnerability

Tolstoy and the author of Ecclesiastes were right in one respect: the meaningfulness of our activities is vulnerable. It depends on our ability to connect with others. But they were wrong to think the inexorable destruction and decay of civilization poses any threat to our ability to assign meaning to our activities now. Those at the end of civilization will be just as able to find value in completing our projects as we are able to find value in starting them.

This might seem like a philosopher's consolation—a departure from the practical-minded focus I have tried to cultivate throughout this book. But I think it is just as relevant to our lives as the retirement advice proffered in Chapter 2. As I finish this book, we are registering the hottest year in recorded history. We have worrying evidence about the rate of environmental degradation and significant uncertainty about humanity's ability to cope with these changes. Morally, we ought to do all we can to protect the generations that will come after us. But environmental degradation also poses a real Doomsday-like threat to value in our lives—in particular our ability to pursue meaning. We need a theory that will empower us to find this kind of value even when humanity's longer-run future is in doubt.

Temporal neutrality stretches us out of the present moment, licensing us to think about how our present plans fit with our futures and with

[23] In Scheffler (2010) he distinguishes between the forward-looking and backward-looking ways that participation in a tradition might confer value on activities. The theory there is relatively temporally neutral, which makes it all the more surprising he explicitly endorses future bias about meaning in Scheffler (2013).

our pasts. It also stretches us out of the confines of what we can now control. And as we have just seen, temporal neutrality even stretches us out of the confines of our own lives. If we want to pursue activities that are not only happy but meaningful, we have to think about how our activities connect with the meaningful projects of others. But—and this is the key idea of this final chapter—we need not stretch *infinitely* far to find meaning. Even finite organisms like us, with finite projects, in a civilization with a humblingly finite history, have plenty of resources now to realize this distinct kind of value.

Bibliography

Adams, R. (1979) 'Existence, Self-Interest, and the Problem of Evil'. *Nous* 13: 53–65.

Adams, R. M. (1989) 'Time and Thisness'. In *Themes from Kaplan*, edited by H. W. Joseph Almog, John Perry, and Howard Wettstein, 23–42. Oxford: Oxford University Press.

Adams, R. M. (2010) *Meaning in Life and Why it Matters*, chap. Comment, 75–84. Princeton: Princeton University Press.

Ainslie, G., and N. Halsam (1992) 'Hyperbolic Discounting'. In *Choice over Time*, edited by G. Loewenstein and J. Elster, 57–92. New York: Russell Sage Foundation.

Albrecht, G., and P. Devlieger (1999) 'The Disability Paradox: High Quality of Life against All Odds'. *Social Science & Medicine* 48: 977–88.

Arntzenius, F. (2008) 'No Regrets, or: Edith Piaf Revamps Decision Theory'. *Erkenntnis* 68: 277–97.

Arntzenius, F., A. Elga, and J. Hawthorne (2004) 'Bayesianism, Infinite Decisions, and Binding'. *Mind* 113: 251–83.

Barrett, L. F. (2017) *How Emotions Are Made*. New York: Houghton Mifflin Harcourt.

Baumeister, R. F., T. F. Heatherton, and D. M. Tice (1994) *Losing Control: How and Why People Fail at Self-Regulation*. Cleveland: Academic Press (Elsevier).

Baumeister, R. F., and J. Tierney (2011) *Willpower: Rediscovering the Greatest Human Strength*. New York: Penguin.

Baumeister, R. F., K. D. Vohs, J. Aaker, and E. N. Garbinsky (2013) 'Some Key Differences between a Happy Life and a Meaningful Life'. *Journal of Positive Psychology* 8: 505–16.

Bentham, J. (1988) *The Principles of Morals and Legislation*. New York: Prometheus Books.

Bradley, B. (2011) 'Narrativity, Freedom and Redeeming the Past'. *Social Theory and Practice* 37: 47–62.

Bratman, M. (1987) *Intention, Plans, and Practical Reason*. Cambridge: Harvard University Press.

Brentano, F. (1973) *The Foundation and Construction of Ethics*. New York: Humanities Press.

Brink, D. O. (2003) 'Prudence and Authenticity: Intrapersonal Conflicts of Value'. *Philosophical Review* 112: 215–45.

Brink, D. O. (2010) 'Prospects for Temporal Neutrality'. In *The Oxford Handbook of Philosophy of Time*, edited by C. Callender, 353–81. Oxford: Clarendon Press.

Broad, C. (1923) *Scientific Thought*. London: Routledge and Kegan Paul, Ltd.

Broome, J. (2004) *Weighing Lives*. Oxford: Oxford University Press.

Buchak, L. (Forthcoming) 'Decision Theory'. In *The Oxford Handbook of Probability and Philosophy*. Oxford: Oxford University Press.

Cahalan, S. (2013) *Brain on Fire: My Month of Madness*. New York: Simon and Schuster.

Caruso, E. M., D. T. Gilbert, and T. D. Wilson (2008) 'A Wrinkle in Time: Asymmetric Valuation of Past and Future Events'. *Psychological Science* 19: 796–801.

Craig, W. L. (1994) *Reasonable Faith: Christian Truth and Apologetics*. Wheaton, IL: Crossway Books.

Crisp, T. (2003) 'Presentism'. In *The Oxford Handbook of Metaphysics*, edited by M. J. Loux and D. W. Zimmerman, 211–46. Oxford: Oxford University Press.

Darwin, C. (1896) *The Expression of the Emotions in Man and Animals*. New York: Harper Collins.

Deigh, J. (1994) 'Cognitivism in the Theory of Emotions'. *Ethics* 104: 824–54.

Dougherty, T. (2011) 'On Whether to Prefer Pain to Pass'. *Ethics* 121: 521–37.

Dougherty, T. (2015) 'Future-Bias and Practical Reason'. *Philosophers' Imprint* 15: 1–16.

Duckworth, A. (2016) *Grit: The Power of Passion and Perseverance*. New York: Scribner.

Duhigg, C. (2016) *Smarter, Faster, Better: The Secrets of Being Productive in Life and Business*. New York: Random House.

Finochiarro, P., and M. Sullivan (2016) 'Yet Another "Epicurean" Argument'. *Philosophical Perspectives* 30: 135–59.

Fleischacker, S. (2015) 'Adam Smith's Moral and Political Philosophy'. *Stanford Encyclopedia of Philosophy*, URL http://plato.stanford.edu/entries/smith-moral-political/.

Flynn, S. M. (2011) *Economics for Dummies*. Indianapolis: Wiley.

Forrest, P. (2006) 'General Facts, Physical Necessity, and the Metaphysics of Time'. *Oxford Studies in Metaphysics* 2: 137–54.

Frank, R. (1988) *Passions within Reason: The Strategic Role of Emotions*. New York: Norton.

Frijda, N. H. (1988) 'The Laws of Emotion'. *American Psychologist* 43: 349–58.

Gabler, N. (2016) 'The Secret Shame of Middle-Class Americans'. *The Atlantic*, May: 52–63.

Gawande, A. (2014) *Being Mortal*. London: Profile Books.

Gilbert, D. (2006) *Stumbling on Happiness*. New York: Vintage Books.

Greene, P. (MS) 'Time Bias, Social Bias, and Value'.

Greene, P., and M. Sullivan (2015) 'Against Time Bias'. *Ethics* 125: 1–24.

Hagger, M. S., and N. L. Chatzisarantis (2016) 'A Multilab Preregistered Replication of the Ego-Depletion Effect'. *Perspectives on Psychological Science* 11: 546–73.

Hare, C. (2008) 'A Puzzle about Other-Directed Time-Bias'. *Australasian Journal of Philosophy* 86: 269–77.

Harman, E. (2009) '"I'll Be Glad I Did It" Reasoning and the Significance of Future Desires'. *Philosophical Perspectives* 23: 177–99.

Heathwood, C. (2008) 'Fitting Attitudes and Welfare'. *Oxford Studies in Metaethics* 3: 47–73.

Hedden, B. (2015a) 'Options and Diachronic Tragedy'. *Philosophy and Phenomenological Research* XC: 423–51.

Hedden, B. (2015b) *Reasons without Persons*. Oxford: Oxford University Press.

Hershfield, H. E., D. G. Goldstein, W. F. Sharpe, J. Fox, L. Yeykelis, L. L. Carstensen, and J. N. Bailenson (2011) 'Increasing Saving Behavior through Age-Progressed Renderings of the Future Self'. *Journal of Marketing Research* 48: S23–S27.

Holton, R. (2009) *Willing, Wanting, Waiting*. Oxford: Oxford University Press.

Horwich, P. (1992) *Asymmetries in Time*. Cambridge: The MIT Press.

Hume, D. (2000) *A Treatise of Human Nature*. Oxford: Oxford University Press.

Hurka, T. (1996) *Perfectionism*. Oxford: Oxford University Press.

Irwin, T. (2007) *The Development of Ethics: A Historical and Critical Study*, vol. I. Oxford: Oxford University Press.

Isaacson, W. (2007) *Einstein: His Life and Universe*. New York: Simon and Schuster.

Jeffrey, R. (1983) *The Logic of Decision*. Chicago: University of Chicago Press, 2nd ed.

Joyce, J. M. (1999) *The Foundations of Causal Decision Theory*. Cambridge: Cambridge University Press.

Kahane, G. (2014) 'Our Cosmic Insignificance'. *Nous* 48: 745–72.

Kahneman, D. (2011) *Thinking, Fast and Slow*. New York: Farrar, Straus, and Giroux.

Kahneman, D., B. L. Frederickson, C. Schreiber, and D. A. Redelmeirer (1993) 'When More Pain Is Preferred to Less: Adding a Better End'. *Psychological Science* 4: 401–5.

Kahneman, D., J. L. Knetsch, and R. H. Thaler (1990) 'Experimental Tests of the Endowment Effect and the Coase Theorem'. *Journal of Political Economy* 98: 1325–48.

Kane, R. (2005) *A Contemporary Introduction to Free Will*. New York: Oxford University Press.

Kavka, G. (1983) 'The Toxin Puzzle'. *Analysis* 43: 33–6.

Kelly, T. (2004) 'Sunk Costs, Rationality, and Acting for the Sake of the Past'. *Nous* 38: 60–85.

Kelly, T. (2014) 'Evidence Can Be Permissive'. In *Contemporary Debates in Epistemology*, edited by M. Steup, J. Turri, and E. Sosa, 298–311. Malden, MA: Wiley-Blackwell, 2nd ed.

Kim, A. (2015) 'Why You Can't Afford to Retire'. *The Washington Monthly*, October 21.

Koopmans, T. (1965) 'Objectives, Constraints, and Outcomes in Optimal Growth Models'. *Econometrica* 35: 1–15.

Korsgaard, C. M. (1989) 'Personal Identity and the Unity of Agency: A Kantian Response to Parfit'. *Philosophy and Public Affairs* 18: 101–32.

Korsgaard, C. M. (2009) *Self-Constitution: Agency, Identity, and Integrity*. Oxford: Oxford University Press.

Krulwich, R. (2014) 'Glenn Gould in Rapture'. URL http://www.radiolab.org/story/glenn-gould-rapture-kw/.

Lewis, C. I. (1955) *The Ground and Nature of the Right*. New York: Columbia University Press.

Lewis, D. (1976) 'Survival and Identity'. In *The Identities of Persons*, edited by A. O. Rorty, 17–40. Berkeley: University of California Press.

Lewis, D. (1979) 'Attitudes *De Dicto* and *De Se*'. *Philosophical Review* 88: 513–43.

Lewis, D. (1986) *On the Plurality of Worlds*. Oxford: Blackwell Publishing.

List, C., and P. Pettit (2013) *Group Agency: The Possibility, Design, and Status of Corporate Agents*. Oxford: Oxford University Press.

Locke, J. (1975) *An Essay Concerning Human Understanding*. Oxford: Oxford University Press.

Loewenstein, G., and J. Elster, eds. (1992) *Choice over Time*. New York: Russell Sage Foundation.

Loomes, G., and R. Sugden (1982) 'Regret Theory: An Alternative Theory of Rational Choice under Uncertainty'. *The Economic Journal* 92: 805–24.

Lord, E., and B. Maguire (2016) *Weighing Reasons*. Oxford: Oxford University Press.

Maclaurin, J., and H. Dyke (2002) " 'Thank Goodness That's Over": The Evolutionary Story'. *Ratio* 15(3): 276–92.

McMahan, J. (2002) *The Ethics of Killing: Problems at the Margins of Life*. Oxford: Oxford University Press.

McTaggart, J. (1927) *The Nature of Existence*. Cambridge: Cambridge University Press.

Markosian, N. (2004) 'A Defense of Presentism'. In *Oxford Studies in Metaphysics*, edited by D. W. Zimmerman, vol. 1, 47–82. Oxford: Oxford University Press.

Meacham, C. J. (2013) 'Impermissive Bayesianism'. *Erkenntnis* 79: 1185–1217.

Merricks, T. (2007) *Truth and Ontology*. Oxford: Oxford University Press.

Merricks, T. (2022) *Self and Identity*. Oxford: Oxford University Press.

Mill, J. (1863) *Utilitarianism*. London: Parker, Son, and Bourne.

Mischel, W. (2014) *The Marshmallow Test*. New York: Little, Brown and Company.

Moore, G. (1903) *Principia Ethica*. Cambridge: Cambridge University Press.

Nagel, T. (1970a) 'Death'. *Mind* 4: 73–80.

Nagel, T. (1970b) *The Possibility of Altruism*. Oxford: Clarendon Press.

Nagel, T. (1979) 'Moral Luck'. In *Mortal Questions*, 24–38. Cambridge: Cambridge University Press.

Nakamura, J., and M. Csikszentmihalyi (2002) 'The Concept of Flow'. In *The Handbook of Positive Psychology*, edited by C. Snyder and S. J. Lopez, 89–105. Oxford: Oxford University Press.

Newman, G. E., P. Bloom, and J. Knobe (2014) 'Value Judgments and the True Self'. *Personality and Social Psychology Bulletin* 40: 203–16.

Nolan, D. (2006) 'Selfless Desires'. *Philosophy and Phenomenological Research* 73: 665–79.

Nozick, R. (1981) *Philosophical Explanations*. Cambridge: Harvard University Press.

Nozick, R. (1993) *The Nature of Rationality*. Princeton: Princeton University Press.

Parfit, D. (1971) 'Personal Identity'. *The Philosophical Review* 80: 3–27.

Parfit, D. (1984) *Reasons and Persons*. Oxford: Clarendon Press.

Parfit, D. (1999) 'Experiences, Subjects and Conceptual Schemes'. *Philosophical Topics* 26: 217–70.

Paul, L. (2014) *Transformative Experience*. Oxford: Oxford University Press.

Perry, J. (1979) 'The Problem of the Essential Indexical'. *Nous* 13: 3–21.

Plato (1997) 'Protagoras'. In *Plato: Complete Works*, edited by J. M. Cooper, 746–90. Indianapolis: Hackett Publishing Company.

Plutchik, R. (1980) *Emotion: A Psychoevolutionary Synthesis*. New York: Harper and Row.

Price, H. (1996) *Time's Arrow and Archimedes' Point: New Directions for the Physics of Time*. Oxford: Oxford University Press.

Prior, A. (1967) *Past, Present, and Future*. Oxford: Clarendon Press.

Pronin, E., C. Y. Olivola, and K. A. Kennedy (2008) 'Doing unto Future Selves as You Would Do unto Others: Psychological Distance and Decision Making'. *Personality and Social Psychology Bulletin* 34: 224–36.

Quine, W. (1950) 'Identity, Ostension, and Hypostasis'. *The Journal of Philosophy* 47: 621–33.

Raphael, D. (2007) *The Impartial Spectator: Adam Smith's Moral Philosophy*. Oxford: Clarendon Press.

Rawls, J. (1971) *A Theory of Justice*. Cambridge: Harvard University Press.

Russell, B. (1915) 'On the Experience of Time'. *The Monist* 25: 212–33.

Scheffler, S. (2010) 'The Normativity of Tradition'. In *Equality and Tradition: Questions of Value in Moral and Political Theory*, 287–311. Oxford: Oxford University Press.

Scheffler, S. (2013) *Death and the Afterlife*. Oxford: Oxford University Press.

Schlesinger, G. (1975) 'The Stillness of Time and Philosophical Equanimity'. *Philosophical Studies* 30: 145–59.

Seneca (1997) *On the Shortness of Life*, translated by C. D. N. Costa. New York: Penguin Classics.

Shiffrin, S. V. (2013) 'Preserving the Valued or Preserving Valuing?' In *Death and the Afterlife*, edited by N. Kolodny, 143–58. Oxford: Oxford University Press.

Sider, T. (1996) 'All the World's a Stage'. *Australasian Journal of Philosophy* 74: 433–53.

Sider, T. (2001) *Four-Dimensionalism: An Ontology of Persistence and Time*. Oxford: Oxford University Press.

Sidgwick, H. (1884) *The Methods of Ethics*. London: Macmillan and Co.

Skow, B. (2015) *Objective Becoming*. Oxford: Oxford University Press.

Smith, A. (1976) *The Theory of Moral Sentiments*. Oxford: Oxford University Press.

Street, S. (2009) 'In Defense of Future Tuesday Indifference: Ideally Coherent Eccentrics and the Contingency of What Matters'. *Philosophical Issues* 19: 273–98.

Sturge-Apple, M. L., J. H. Suor, P. T. Davies, D. Cicchetti, M. A. Skibo, and F. A. Rogosch (2016) 'Vagal Tone and Children's Delay of Gratification: Differential Sensitivity in Resource-Poor and Resource-Rich Environments'. *Psychological Science* 27: 885–93.

Suhler, C., and C. Callender (2012) 'Thank Goodness That Argument Is Over: Explaining the Temporal Value Asymmetry'. *Philosopher's Imprint* 12: 1–16.

Sullivan, M. (2012a) 'The Minimal A-Theory'. *Philosophical Studies* 158: 149–74.

Sullivan, M. (2012b) 'Problems for Temporary Existence in Tense Logic'. *Philosophy Compass* 7: 43–57.

Sullivan, M. (Forthcoming a) 'Personal Volatility'. *Philosophical Issues*.

Sullivan, M. (Forthcoming b) 'A Philosophy for the End (Whenever It Comes)'. *Georgetown Journal of Law and Public Policy*.

Sullivan, P. (2016) 'Want to Keep New Year's Resolutions? Consider the Consequences of Failing'. *The New York Times*, January 1.

Taylor, R. (2000) *Good and Evil*. Amherst, NY: Prometheus Books.

Temkin, L. S. (2012) *Rethinking the Good: Moral Ideals and the Nature of Practical Reasoning*. Oxford: Oxford University Press.

Thaler, R. H., and C. R. Sunstein (2009) *Nudge: Improving Decisions about Health, Wealth and Happiness*. New York: Penguin.

Tobia, K. P. (2015) 'Personal Identity and the Phineas Gage Effect'. *Analysis* 75: 396–405.

Tolstoy, L. (1987) *A Confession and Other Religious Writings*. London: Penguin Books.

Tversky, A., and D. Kahneman (1981) 'The Framing of Decision and the Psychology of Choice'. *Science* 211: 453–8.

Ubel, P. A., G. Loewenstein, N. Schwarz, and D. Smith (2005) 'Misimagining the Unimaginable: The Disability Paradox and Health Care Decision Making'. *Health Psychology (Suppl)* 24: S57–S62.

Velleman, J. D. (1991) 'Well-Being and Time'. *Pacific Philosophical Quarterly* 72: 48–77.

Velleman, J. D. (1996) 'Self to Self'. *The Philosophical Review* 105: 39–76.

Vonnegut, K. (1969) *Slaughterhouse Five (or The Children's Crusade)*. New York: Dell Publishing.

Warren, J. (2004) *Facing Death: Epicurus and His Critics*. Oxford: Oxford University Press.

Warren, J. (2014) *The Pleasures of Reason in Plato, Aristotle, and the Hellenistic Hedonists*. Cambridge: Harvard University Press.

Weber, E., E. Johnson, H. Chang, J. Brodscholl, and D. Goldstein (2007) 'Asymmetric Discounting in Intertemporal Choice: A Query-Theory Account'. *Psychological Science* 18: 516–23.

Weller, C. (2004) 'Scratched Fingers, Ruined Lives, and Lesser Goods'. *Hume Studies* 30: 51–86.

White, R. (2014) 'Evidence Cannot Be Permissive'. In *Contemporary Debates in Epistemology*, edited by M. Steup, J. Turri, and E. Sosa, 312–23. Malden, MA: Wiley-Blackwell, 2nd ed.

Whiting, J. (1986) 'Friends and Future Selves'. *The Philosophical Review* 95: 547–80.

Williams, B. (1970) 'The Self and the Future'. *The Philosophical Review* 79: 161–80.

Wilson, B. (2015) *First Bite: How We Learn to Eat*. New York: Basic Books.

Wilson, M., and M. Daly (2004) 'Do Pretty Women Inspire Men to Discount the Future?' *Proceedings of the Royal Society: Biology Letters* S177–S179.

Wolf, S. (1986) 'Self-Interest and Interest in Selves'. *Ethics* 96: 704–20.

Wolf, S. (2010) *Meaning in Life and Why It Matters*. Princeton: Princeton University Press.

Yeats, W. B. (1996) 'Calvary (1921)'. In *Selected Poems and Four Plays*, edited by M. Rosenthal, 94–101. New York: Scribner, 4th ed.

Zimmerman, D. (1998) 'Temporary Intrinsics and Presentism'. In *Metaphysics: The Big Questions*, edited by P. van Inwagen and D. W. Zimmerman, 206–18. Oxford: Blackwell.

Zimmerman, D. W. (2005) 'The A-Theory of Time, the B-Theory of Time, and "Taking Tense Seriously"'. *Dialectica* 59: 401–57.

Index of Key Terms and Authors

Thought Experiment Index